Study: Revised

Your roadmap to exam success

Jon Dunckley

Contents

For all the teachers who devote their lives to helping others learn. And especially for Madeline, who has taught me so much about life and love.

Foreword

As education providers in the Financial Planning Profession, we are thrilled to introduce "Study: Revised" to our community. This book is a game-changer for the financial planning profession, addressing a critical need: efficient and effective study techniques for aspiring and advancing financial planners.

At NextGen Planners, we've long championed the philosophy of "study less, pass more." This approach isn't about cutting corners; it's about maximising the efficiency of your learning process.

The techniques outlined in this book are at the core of our methodology, which has helped countless professionals in our community achieve their qualifications more quickly and with less stress.

The financial planning landscape is constantly evolving, and with it, the demands on our knowledge and skills. As professionals, we're expected to maintain a high level of expertise while balancing client work, business management, and personal lives.

This makes effective study techniques not just helpful, but

essential. Study: Revised breaks down the learning process into manageable sections, from initial planning to exam preparation. This structured approach aligns perfectly with our NextGen Planners Academy, where we emphasise modern learning techniques and practical skills alongside exam preparation.

What I particularly appreciate about this book is its focus on understanding how the mind works and tailoring study methods accordingly. This cognitive approach to learning is something we've seen yield remarkable results in our community. It's not just about memorising facts; it's about developing a deep understanding that can be applied in real-world financial planning scenarios.

The book's emphasis on effective note taking, purposeful revision, and exam-specific strategies resonates strongly with our "study less, pass more" philosophy. These techniques help our members not only pass exams but truly grasp the material, setting them up for long-term success in their careers. As financial planners, our ultimate goal is to provide the best possible service to our clients. By mastering these study techniques, you're not just preparing for exams; you're laying the groundwork for a career of continuous learning and excellence in financial planning.

I encourage every aspiring and practicing financial planner to embrace the methods in this book. Whether you're working towards your initial qualifications or advancing to higher levels, these techniques will serve you well throughout your career.

At NextGen Planners, we're committed to empowering the future of financial planning. "Study: Revised" is an invaluable tool in this mission, helping to create more knowledgeable, efficient, and confident professionals in our field.

Adam Carolan
CEO NextGen Planners

Introduction

"A journey of a thousand miles begins with a single step"
Lao Tzu
"Let's get this party started" *Pink*

Hello! Thanks for being here. I'm Jon, your guide through the wonders of study.

If you're as shrewd as I think you are, you'll probably want some proof of concept and want to know why you should listen to what I have to say before you go any further. Quite right too.

Never take anything at face value – your time is valuable. If someone's asking you to invest that time, make sure it's going to be worth it. (Good news, by knowing that you're already on the right tracks for study success).

Let me start by introducing myself properly. I could share my age but that's not helping anyone, least of all me, so instead, here's my exam-sitting background:

- The first exams I remember taking are my primary school tests when I was 8. I haven't stopped since.

- So far, I've passed 10 GCSEs, 3 A-Levels, an undergraduate degree, a master's degree, and I'm working on another master's right now.
- I've also obtained three degree-level professional qualifications (all linked to my original career in financial services).

That's over 40 years of exams and the equivalent of six degrees... You'd think I'd have had enough by now, wouldn't you?

Of course, simply taking exams isn't the same as knowing how to pass them effectively. That's where my undergraduate degree comes in. It was in psychology and it's a subject I've never stopped studying. There's something fascinating about the way the brain works and learning how to get the most from it. And that interest, along with a lot of practical experience, is what's led to you reading this book.

As well as taking my own exams, I've supported hundreds of people through theirs as a tutor in financial services. And I work with other tutors across various disciplines daily. So, this book is my attempt to transfer the collective knowledge from me, them, and the world of psychology, to as many people as possible, and help you smash through whichever exam(s) you're currently facing.

As you continue reading, you'll find a combination of:

- My own knowledge and experience. Things I've found to help me and my students over the years. Much trial and error has been involved, and I'll help you skip straight to the learns.
- Insight and advice from my company's advisory board. Comprising teachers and educators, these people spend all day imparting knowledge to

children and young people, across the widest range of topics. They've shared what works and what doesn't, so you can get the benefit for your own studies.

- Findings from academic research. This isn't a stuffy textbook, but it's good to know there's science to back up what I'm saying. It also makes me feel less sad for the authors. (Did you know the average academic journal article is read by only 9 people? All that work, all that knowledge, just sitting there gathering electronic dust. So, I've made it a nice round 10 for the lucky few).

Reading this book will offer you practical experience, based on scientific principles, with a human touch and a bit of humour along the way. I've kept it deliberately light, and relatively short, so you don't have to spend weeks studying how to study. What a nightmare that would be.

There is, however, one unfortunate truth you need to keep in mind. Sadly, simply buying a book on study technique isn't the same thing as *developing* study technique.

You need to work through this book and implement at least some of the suggestions into your own study practice. Nothing will make its way into your head through osmosis. I know, I've tried. Cognitive neuroscience exam, 1995 - no matter how long I left the textbook on my table, the knowledge never made its way to my brain until I opened the blasted book.

Thankfully, I did open it in the end, and I'll be using some of the most important bits in chapter one.

So, bottom line? ***This book won't help you if you don't use it.***

To balance that hammer blow, though, if you do follow the

tips and techniques outlined, you'll have a cracking chance of passing.

It's your decision

The goal of this book is to help you approach your exam knowing exactly what's ahead of you. You'll be going in fully equipped for the task in hand, brimming with confidence for the pass, and knowing the information can be retrieved and applied from your head at will. Sounds like a win, right? Good.

Then, before you do anything else, you need to acknowledge one thing:

Every minute you spend studying is a choice.

You could be spending it with your family, with friends, playing video games, doing sport, or whatever else you fancy. You're giving up those things for your study. That puts both a price on your time and a duty to use it wisely.

So, having decided to study, how are you going to get exam success? Well, passing an exam requires two things:

1. acquiring the knowledge, and
2. keeping it in your brain long enough for it to serve its purpose.

This book looks at both elements separately but, in reality, they're two overlapping parts of the journey. How you gather information effectively is an important skill whether you're doing an exam or writing a coursework essay. How you make sure it sticks in your mind is more important for the exam.

How this book works

To make sure you can cover the key points, the book's broken down into five sections:

1. **Getting going** – before you even start studying, it's helpful to understand how the mind works and use this knowledge to form a plan of attack. This means knowing what will be expected of you in the exam and making sure you're doing the right things. You know what they say – fail to plan, plan to fail. Let's not fall down that hole, eh?

2. **Download and store** – this is all about how you read and make notes effectively (Hint: re-writing the textbook by hand isn't the best way). You'll also find advice on how to approach coursework and essay assignments.

3. **The big day approaches** – the closer the exam is, the more important it is for you to follow the plan and to revise with purpose. You'll find a dozen techniques outlined which might help – they've certainly helped me over the years.

4. **Taming the beast** – this section is split into three chapters. Exam preparation for all exams, then specific chapters for both multiple choice and written exams. Different techniques apply to each, so you'll need to look at them separately.

5. **Pulling it all together** – finally there are pointers from other students, and sources of further reading, if you're interested in learning more. Just to be clear – that isn't me saying you should read to procrastinate. The point is to pass the exam, so explore more about techniques that might help, but

don't disappear down rabbit holes - becoming an expert on study is all very well and good but if that means you've no time to revise it might not be your best plan of attack. You've been warned.

Each chapter starts with a guide to what it covers and ends with a 'too long; didn't read' summary. On the one hand, that might seem like overkill but there's method in the madness.

There's a quote often attributed to Aristotle (though no-one really knows who said it), 'Tell them what you're going to tell them, tell them, then tell them what you've told them!" This is used by trainers the world over because it aids memory.

In this book, it also serves another purpose. It allows you to be selective and to make best use of your valuable time.

Using the introductions and summaries, you can work out whether a particular chapter's useful to you. Don't waste your time with things from which you'll get no value. So, if you read the chapter introduction and you're not sure, flick to the end and look at the summary.

If it doesn't seem relevant, leave it, and move on to the next chapter. (I won't be offended). Sometimes study calls for you to be ruthless... even to me. There's no rush to read a chapter on coursework and essays if you're only being examined by multiple choice exam. Instead, go back to it next time when essays form part of the requirement.

Ultimately, there's no right or wrong way to study, just the way that works best for you. What I'm trying to do here is give you the tools to help you find your own 'brain-friendly' study solution. And the secret is to give things a go.

If you love something, and it transforms your study, keep it. If you don't, bin it. Through that kind of trial and error you can build up the ultimate toolkit for your own brain. And the real beauty? Once you've got it in place, your toolkit will last you a lifetime!

I really hope you enjoy this book and take from it what you need. I've enjoyed writing it and honestly believe it has the potential to help you achieve success.

Good luck with your studies.

Jon Dunckley
February 2024

1. Getting going

Chapter 1

Understanding memory

"Life is all memory, except for the one present moment that goes by you so quickly you hardly catch it going." Tennessee Williams

"I remember don't worry. How could I ever forget..." Phil Collins, In the air tonight.

What's in this chapter?

THIS CHAPTER's all about how the memory works. You'll see how the short-term and long-term memory have vastly different capacities, and you'll look at some basic memory building techniques. You'll also see why learning styles, although often talked about, are much less important to your study success than you might think. The aim of this chapter is to give you all the background and context you need as you go through the rest of the book.

Your brain is incredible

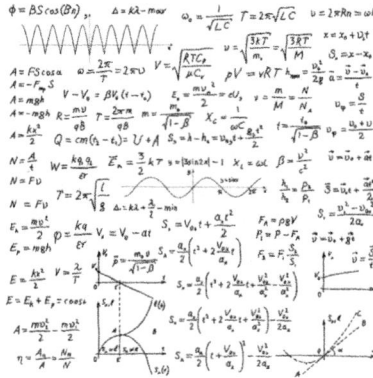

The human brain's a powerful thing. Some people argue it's the most complex thing in the known universe. Each of us has around 100 billion brain cells, every one of which is able to connect to thousands of others. That adds up to trillions of different connections, all working seamlessly every minute of the day.

A trillion can be just too big a number to relate to, so let's put it a slightly different way. Just one cubic millimetre of your brain can have up to one billion connections, and there are a lot of cubic millimetres. In fact, if you unfolded the grey wrinkly bit on the outside of your brain (the cerebral cortex if you want to be all technical about it) it would be about the size of a broadsheet newspaper. It just wrinkles so you can pack in a huge amount of processing power. Amazing! [1].

Common myth says we humans only use a fraction of our brains. The reality, however, seems to be we use it all very effectively, but we can always do better. I say 'seems to be' because despite our best endeavours, we still know very little about the mechanics of the brain. Luckily, thanks to brain scans we're learning more all the time and there's a huge amount of research on the subject.

The field of cognitive neuroscience (or, in simple terms, the study of the biological processes that lead to knowledge and learning) is giving us more insight into the operation of the brain, and how to make the best of it. So, these are the edited highlights to help you become a better learner.

Structure of memory

It isn't possible to look at everything the brain does. So how it translates sound into language, or how you interpret what you see, for instance, can wait for another time. Instead, the focus here is primarily on your memory and how your brain builds and recalls memories – that's the good stuff if you want to pass exams.

So, let's start with the basics. You effectively have three forms of memory working together:

1. **Immediate memory** – this is very short-term in nature. It can hold things for 10-20 seconds in your conscious awareness. In other words, this is the 'in one ear, and out the other' form of memory. It'll keep things, deal with them, or forget them. It's what you'd call your general awareness.

2. **Working memory** – if you were a computer, this would be the documents open on your desktop at any one time. You can't hold much in that working memory; this is just where things go when you're actively using them. Estimates vary but research suggests you can hold 5 to 9 items or 'chunks' at a time. 'Chunks' allow you to group

things into a single 'item'. So, for example, a telephone number beginning with 020 wouldn't take up three items – you'd remember 020 as a single chunk. That said, even if you're remembering chunks you're still not talking about much storage.

3. **Long-term memory** – this one is vast! Nobody knows quite how vast we're talking, but it's substantial. (Not surprising given the number of cells in the brain). One analogy is that the brain is like a Sky TV box with a big enough capacity to record over 100-years of continuous television. If your short-term memory is the documents on your computer desktop, the long-term memory is your cloud storage, and you've got a lot of it!

Some people have super-charged long-term memory due to a condition called 'hyperthymesia' [2] which allows them to remember, in great detail, pretty much every event in their life. What did they have for lunch on the 22 March 2018, for example? If you ask them, they'll tell you! Now, that's not necessarily a positive thing. There's a value in being able to forget when we want to. If you fall over and break your leg, you need the pain signals to tell you to get help and then, for most people, your brain has grown very skilled at actively forgetting things for your own benefit. After all, you don't want to remember that pain every day for the rest of your life.

It's also good to forget learning at times – at least temporarily. Your ability to speak English might be natural, but you need to forget that natural recall briefly when you're trying to learn another language. When you get your picture taken in your French class you want to say 'fromage' instead of 'cheese', so your brain needs to suppress the memory of the word 'cheese' being associated with picture taking. If it's Spanish class, you'll be looking for 'queso'.

When you need to do something with your memories – use them for an exam for instance - you have to fire them back up onto your desktop. That means bringing them back into working memory, and this is really important, as you'll see when you look at exam technique in chapter nine.

If your brain is preoccupied worrying about the exam, or anything else outside that exam, it'll limit the amount you can process in your working memory. And you'll find it harder to access all the information you need from your own 'cloud storage'.

Spam filters

Before moving on to thinking about how the brain actually stores and retrieves information, it's worth pointing out your brain has an absolutely astonishing spam filter. In fact, if you could get one for your computer that was half as good, you'd be happy.

In every instant, there are millions of items of data around you. Your brain can only process around 40 of those at once, so it just filters out everything else. It automatically gets rid of almost everything you encounter.

Most of the time that's great. You don't need to pay conscious attention to the sound of your kids recording their latest TikTok video, or the latest drama playing out on the TV. You can let those things happen in the house while you're occupied with other things.

The goal of good study, though, is to make sure the things you want to remember make it through your spam filter and get stored – and that's where the skill comes in! Hang around in this book to learn how.

Storage and retrieval

So, you know the brain is complex. One of the key questions many people ask is, 'Which part of the brain is responsible for memory?'

Well, think of your brain anatomy like an apple – a core, middle flesh, and outer skin [1]. These parts need to work in harmony, like musicians in a band. If they're all playing the same tune, you get a rock classic. If they're not, you get a bad year six end of term concert (and, if you've ever been to one, you'll know that's really not a positive thing!).

Deep beneath the 'skin' of the apple - the grey wrinkly bit (the cerebral cortex, you'll recall) there's a part of the more primal brain called the hippocampus. In our apple analogy, this is part of the core and it's essential for forming new memories. Memories don't live inside the hippocampus, but without it, new memories don't get stored. So, imagine it's like an office assistant who regularly files things away.

How do we know this? Well, one poor chap, Henry Molaison, had his hippocampus removed by a surgeon who was trying to solve his epilepsy. While it did fix that problem, it resulted in his inability to lay down new memories [3]. The researcher who studied him met with him every couple of weeks and it was like he was meeting her for the first time. He would introduce himself all over again and take great interest in why she'd come to see him – even though she'd been coming regularly for years.

Since Henry, neuroscientists have been able to demonstrate the significant role the hippocampus plays in the creation of memory. When you want to remember something, your brain passes it to the memory, it gets encoded through the hippocampus, and is then distributed around the brain.

Your memories aren't stored within one single area of your

brain. Instead, the parts of the memory are passed to the different centres of the brain responsible for the relevant information. Visual memories are stored in the 'occipital lobe', auditory memories in the 'temporal lobe' and more tactile memories in the 'motor cortex'. These different areas then link together in a 'neural network' representing that memory.

Each time we want to remember something, our brain goes out to all the parts involved in the memory and asks it to send a report. In other words, it fires up the network. The 'reports' that get sent are like pieces of jigsaw and the brain uses those to reassemble the memory. So not every one of the connections involved in the network fires up every time you recall a memory. As a result, the areas responsible send slightly different jigsaw pieces, and the finished picture changes a little each time.

Interestingly, those re-formed memories then go on to shape how the picture will look if you recall it again later – your memory actually gets changed by your memory! The stronger the connections you've formed, the quicker the brain gathers the jigsaw, and the more vivid the pieces become. In fact, the definition of learning is simply that the neural networks fire quicker on the third time of asking than they did on the first.

You're probably already spotting the opportunities here for your studies. Firstly, if the brain's storing parts of the memory in different areas, could you use all those areas maximum storage power for your study? Well, in short, yes!

Since the brain stores visual information in one place, auditory information in another, and tactile information in a third, if you can interact with the information you want to store in multiple ways, you can create multiple areas of memory. By doing this, the reassembled whole will be more powerful, and that's what you're going to do through this book.

Secondly, if the memory's stronger and more accurate

when more of the neural network fires up, is there a way to make those networks stronger, and get them to fire more readily? Again, 'yes'!

Improving memory

The starting point for improving your memory and achieving exam success is recognising your experience actually changes the structure of your brain. When you remember things, you form new connections and those connections become a part of your brain structure. The stronger they become, the more permanently wired that network is, and your brain alters, however slightly.

This process of shaping the brain is known as 'neuroplasticity' and you can exploit it and make it work for you with concerted effort, even when you're getting old, like me.

In one study [4], researchers scanned the brains of trainee London taxi drivers before and after their training. London's black-cab drivers go through one of the most extensive training processes in the world, known as 'the knowledge'. They're expected to learn the quickest route between any two places given the time of day and likely traffic. They're also required to know all the relevant landmarks in case their passenger knows what it looks like, but not what it's called. In short, the knowledge is intensive.

What these researchers found was that the hippocampus changed size as people underwent the training. The part of the brain marshalling memory got bigger. Subsequent research has built on this and shown, that with applied effort, you can improve the functioning of your memories and positively change the wiring of your brain.

Revisit and reinforce

'Neurons that fire together, wire together'. It's a phrase you'll often hear in psychology circles. In other words, when you fire up neurons in the brain, they develop connections and start to form neural networks. Every time you make them fire together, by recalling a particular memory, the pathways become stronger and the links more solid. Your brain is literally being rewired.

It's a little like a snow-covered field. When the first person walks across it, there are a few footprints. If nobody else walks across, the snow soon fills in those footprints, and it's like they were never there. But if another person walks across soon after the first, the prints get bigger. A third person and it's starting to look more like a track. By the twentieth set of feet, there's a clear pathway through the snow.

When you study, you want to keep walking those pathways, firing up the neural networks so they become stronger; unbreakable even. This process is known as 'reinforcement' and it's the cornerstone of study. The important thing is getting the timing intervals right, so you don't leave it too long and find the snow has covered your tracks.

'Jost's law' [5] says repetition increases the strength of older memories more than recent memories. That sounds a little heavy but let me explain. Jost's law is essentially telling you there's no benefit to reinforcing things you've literally just learned. You need to space out your reinforcement. Let something live in the brain, then revisit it. Wire the neurons together, then leave them for a while, before firing them up again. Get the spacing right and you'll make the connections much stronger.

So, what's the right spacing for reinforcement? Well, there's no absolute consensus, but it seems to be broadly agreed that:

11

- Memory declines fastest in the first 24 hours
- Then slides further over the next 3 weeks, and...
- After 3 weeks it tends to stabilise.

What can you take from this? Well, if you review something after 24 hours and no more than three weeks later, you should have a good chance of retaining it.

Some researchers take this slightly further and put in an extra review at the one-week mark. This is my own favoured approach, and the one I'm going to recommend in this book:

1. Study – to create the neural networks.
2. Review after one day to re-fire those networks and tell the brain this is stuff you want to hang on to.
3. Review again one week later. Yes, brain, I do want it! Don't throw it out.
4. Leave it a further three weeks and come back for another review (one month after you initially learned it).

Of course, this whole process is a month long, so if you don't have a month, you'll need to edit this – perhaps just the one day, and one-week recaps, topped up with pre-exam practice. But, if you've got the time, using one day, one week, one month puts you in great shape for remembering it forever.

Left brain / right brain

You may hear people describe themselves as being 'left-brained' or 'right-brained'. The terms are often used in the same way someone would describe themselves as being left- or right-handed. But what does it mean, and is it scientifically valid?

Well, there's some good science here, but it's often misinterpreted, leading to some dubious conclusions.

It's true the structure of the left side of our brain differs from that of the right. For most people, the left half of the brain is more involved in logical matters. It handles words, letters, and other academic stuff. The right half handles the more creative endeavours. This is where pictures and songs live.

It isn't entirely true to talk of them as being separate. In most tasks, the two sides work together to complete functions, but with each pulling its weight in its favourite area. So the idea of being left- or right-brained is a bit of a myth. In reality, processing occurs across both hemispheres of the brain, and you can help yourself learn more by making good use of what happens on either side.

Work the system

As well as reinforcing specific memories, you'll be trying to give those memories more 'importance' to your brain. The more important the brain regards the information as being, the more it tries to cling to it. The brain's primed to keep things it regards as having meaning, purpose, or relevance, otherwise you'll find it hits the spam filter!

One of the ways you can do this effectively is to create associations. By creating links between the things that you want to remember, and something the memory already holds as important, you increase the 'value' the brain gives the new information. Let's look at how...

Emotion

It's often said there's no learning without emotion. I'm not about to suggest you fall in love with your study text, but you can use emotion to help increase the value of information you study. The most effective way to do this is to create a firm intention to learn. If you're forcing yourself to sit and study, your brain associates the information with negative thoughts and low value. You don't want to be there; you're doing it against your will. Your brain believes this can't be important because your overriding emotions are apathy and even resentment. That won't increase the mental currency of the information.

Instead, create a positive intention to learn. Convince yourself this study session is worthwhile and will help drive you to exam success. Your brain will respond accordingly.

Location

In 1975, a group of divers were asked to read a list of words underwater [6]. Some were then asked to recall the text on dry land, others were asked to recall it underwater. You can guess what happened. The ones on dry land remembered 30% fewer words than those who recalled underwater. This principle (state dependency) suggests you have better recall for information if you're in the same state as you were when you learned it.

So, how does this help you? Well, I'm not suggesting you pop on your breathing apparatus and head out to sea – unless you're planning to take the exam underwater, that is.

You can, however, use this concept to your advantage. If you're planning on sitting the exam at home, using one of the many online services now available, think about doing at least some of your studying at the desk you'll use for the exam.

If you're going into an exam hall, you're unlikely to be sitting on a sofa for your test, so do some of your studying at a desk.

Why am I saying 'some'? Well, there's also benefit in mixing up where you study. It creates powerful associations, known as 'contextual cues', between what you study, and your memories of multiple locations. In other words, you create more neural networks. You can do this in a couple of ways:

1. Study everything in multiple locations – associate all your studying partly with home, partly with the coffee shop, partly with the office etc. Your brain will link that material to your memories of each of those places, firing up more networks.
2. Study different things in different locations – link one topic to the coffee shop, another to the lounge at home, another to the library. Then, in the exam, vividly imagine the location to help prompt the memory.

Trigger songs

This is my very favourite technique, and it draws on similar principles to the use of location.

If you were asked to recite a poem you learned three years ago, you would likely struggle. If you were asked to sing a song from the charts from the same time period, most people would find that a lot easier.

Think about it, each Christmas the same hits come on the radio. You've not heard them for a year, but you can still sing along. I mean, he gave you his heart! What were you thinking giving it away the very next day?!

Music's something you'll come back in chapter eight, but for now, let's introduce one key technique. It's what I call the 'trigger song'.

The trigger song plays on the natural link between memory and music. You pick a song you don't hear very often – an album track, not one of the major singles. Each time you settle down to study, before you start, you play the song. When you finish, you play it again.

Your brain starts to link the song to the material you're studying. Then, on exam day, you play the song a few times while you're getting ready, and away you go. Think of it as a way of warming up your brain's database before you start – just make sure you pick a different song for each exam. Nobody wants a head full of medieval history when you're taking an investment planning exam.

You'll take this principle even further later in the book, but since this technique really needs to be implemented from the start of your study, you can have it now. Don't say I never give you anything.

Sleep

One of the greatest power-ups for your memory is something which requires nothing from you! Sleep.

During the REM (rapid eye movement) stage of sleep, the hippocampus runs around the brain. It reviews the activity of the day, strengthens connections, and generally tidies up. A bit like the clean-up operation that used to take place each night when my kids were younger. We'd get them to sleep, run around picking up the toys, clear away the general carnage and reset for the next day. Just looking after the kids and answering their many questions prevented any tidy-up. The down time once they were sleeping was very much needed!

Your brain is the same. Without sleep, it can't reinforce your memories and strengthen them. It does its best in quiet times of the day when there's little other mental processing going on, but at night is when the real work is done.

As an adult, you should aim for 7 to 9 hours' good sleep each night while you're studying. Spending less time sleeping so you can read more is absolutely a false economy. So, get some study time in before bed and reap the benefits!

Food and drink

Water is life. Literally. It's vital you drink enough as dehydration significantly impairs the brain's abilities. Even modest dehydration can damage performance. You should be shooting for a couple of litres of water every day if you want to keep the brain functioning optimally for your learning.

Likewise, the brain needs food – we need glucose to function. If you've ever exercised hard, you'll know the brain can get quite foggy. That's because your muscles use up all the glucose stores in the body, leaving the brain short. If you're not properly fuelling, you won't get optimal functioning. Don't skip meals. Instead, aim for a 'brain-friendly' diet including vitamins and minerals (a multi-vitamin tablet is a good fall-back) along with fatty acids (like those found in fish).

Exercise

Neurotransmitters are chemicals in the brain which perform essential functions. One of the most important for memory is dopamine. In fact, it's sometimes called the learning chemical because of its role in forming memory. It's released by your old friend the hippocampus to slow random firing in the brain and then help neurons get ready to fire when you want them to.

Dopamine's released when you're doing something new, being rewarded, or taking risks (that's why gamers can concentrate on Call of Duty, but not homework). Increasing dopamine is also associated with better focus in people with Attention Deficit Hyperactivity Disorder (ADHD). And importantly, you can stimulate it through exercise.

That's not all exercise does. It also increases blood flow to the brain, reduces stress (which can impair memory formation and retrieval), and promotes neuroplasticity. Given the huge benefits of exercise, it's one you should grab with both hands. But how? Well, you could look at:

- Listening to podcasts while walking – there are all kinds of podcasts offering learning on diverse topics. Find one relevant to your study and away you go.
- Record your own – get a recorder, put down some notes and play them to yourself when you're out with the dog.
- Pop a YouTube video on the iPad while you're on the exercise bike (this is one I do all the time).

One caveat here, don't try to learn complex subjects while you're doing a hard workout. The act of exercising hard draws blood away from the brain and toward the muscles, so the more you need to concentrate, the lighter the exercise. You just need it to be enough to raise the heart rate a little.

Using this information to promote study

We've already covered so much of the way the brain works. Hopefully it's starting to get you thinking differently about the way you study. Just sitting in the same chair, reading the same book isn't a powerful strategy for learning. You can, and will, do much better. That's why this book's here – to help you really boost your learning and smash through your exams.

Learning styles – the elephant in the room

"But surely, I should just follow my learning style, Jon? I don't need all this, do I?"

Er, well... let's talk about learning styles for a second.

It's one of the more divisive topics in education and stems partly from the 'neuromyth' of left-brain or right-brain dominance. The view of many researchers, including me, is you really don't want to get hung up on it, and here's why.

The most common approach to learning styles was developed by Honey and Mumford [7]. It breaks learners into four groups:

- **Activists** – people who learn best by doing and being hands on.
- **Reflectors** – these people like to look back on their experience and ponder it, they talk things through.
- **Theorists** – this group draws their conclusions after the event, based on a thorough analysis of the evidence.
- **Pragmatists** – people who look at the purpose of the learning and ask, 'what's the point of this?'

Honey and Mumford suggest you should match your study activity to your learning style to have the best chance of retaining the information.

Other approaches look at things slightly differently. For instance, Barbe and colleagues [8] have a theory that how you learn depends on which of their three 'learning modalities' you respond to best:

- **Auditory** – listening to content

- **Visual** – reading or watching content
- **Kinaesthetic** – getting hands on, 'doing' (e.g. role plays).

Other models build on these concepts, adding in different definitions or learning approaches. Yet, as popular as these models have become, the evidence doesn't seem to support their validity. In fact, there's a strong body of evidence to suggest they don't work.

It almost seems the idea of learning styles has been swept into established practice without anyone really looking at whether there was truth in the theory. According to one study, 93% of teachers in the UK agree 'Individuals learn better when they receive information in their preferred learning style' [9]. Unfortunately, 90% of academics also agree there's a 'basic conceptual flaw with learning styles theory,' and only 1/3 of academics in UK higher education actually use learning styles [10].

So why do people cling to the idea of learning styles being effective? Well, for one thing, it plays into the human desire to categorise things. We love to put things into boxes, and learning styles are neat boxes to put people into [11]. Unfortunately, there's no good evidence that learning styles work, nor that the odd learning style questionnaire can achieve this kind of sorting (It isn't quite the Hogwarts Sorting Hat!)

What's the answer?

If you're going to dismiss the idea of learning styles, what can you replace it with? Well, you've seen enough of the anatomy of memory now for you to start to create better alternatives.

In the main, you need to use multiple strategies. Make the brain store information in lots of different ways. The more ways it stores things, the more jigsaw pieces you'll have available on exam day. If you only store details in the visual cortex, and that's missing in action on exam day, you're in trouble. Store it in multiple ways, in multiple areas, and success looks more likely!

My message, then? Don't worry too much about learning styles. Good techniques work for all, and the rest of the book should give you something you can run with. Mix up your learning and learn in multiple ways. The more ways you can get something into your brain the better. So read, listen to lectures, watch videos, write – take things in through multiple channels.

Once you've read about the techniques, try them. Combine them. Find your own blend of study and revision methods. That will always be your most effective approach.

'Too long; didn't read' summary

- The brain's a wonderful and complex thing. Each cubic millimetre of the 'grey stuff' can have up to one billion connections in it.
- Memory can be broken into three parts – your immediate memory (awareness), your working memory (like the documents open on your computer) and your long-term memory (your very own cloud storage).
- The goal of learning is to move things from working memory to your 'cloud', with the ability to recall it at will.
- You achieve this through reinforcement. The more often you fire up the memory, the stronger the connections become. And there are optimum gaps between recaps if you want to get the best from your brain – one day, one week, one month.
- A part of the brain called the hippocampus acts as the controller of memory. It's possible to improve how well the hippocampus functions using good study techniques.
- The idea that someone is 'left-brained' or 'right-brained' is a myth. The left and right sides of the brain do have primary responsibility for different things, but your whole brain's involved in the process of learning.
- You can increase the storage 'currency' of memory by linking it to other things such as locations or emotions. And wanting to study, rather than being forced to, will increase memory too.
- Food, water, sleep, and exercise all play vital roles in the process of learning. If you don't get enough

of any of these, you won't learn as effectively as you could.

- The notion of learning styles lacks scientific rigour, so stop worrying about what yours might or might not be. Instead, make use of multiple learning methods to encourage the brain to store information in many different places. That's what makes it easier to recall later.

Chapter 2

What do you know?

"If you know your enemy and know yourself, you need not fear the result of a hundred battles" Sun Tzu
"Remember, the Boy Scouts motto? (Be prepared) Keep that in mind at all times" Adam West, Batman

What's in this chapter?

HERE, you'll cover the important task of learning *about* the exam before you start learning *for* the exam. You'll consider why it's so important to know the structure, the format, the pass mark (and the pass rate) of the exam. You'll also see the huge value of past papers, if you use them correctly.

It's the day of the final...

Picture the scene. It's the World Cup final, and you're on the pitch. It's the 89th minute. Scores are level. You make a run into the penalty box and you're brought down. The referee's whistle blows, their finger points to the penalty spot. The crowd goes wild. You look to your captain who points right back at you – you won the spot kick, you're taking it. It's OK, you've taken penalties before, you'll be fine.

You calm your nerves, and a hush falls over the crowd. You ready yourself, waiting for the referee's signal. But, before you can take the shot, the referee steps forward and pulls out a blindfold. They put it over your eyes and spin you around – three times clockwise, four times anticlockwise.

You feel dizzy, disoriented, and a little scared. Now the referee blows the whistle to indicate you can take the kick. How would you rate your chances?

In those circumstances, it doesn't matter who you are; you're going to struggle. Unless someone tells you, you won't even know if you're facing the goal anymore, so how can you possibly hit it? Yet many students approach their exams in exactly this way. They have so little idea of what's expected of them, they might as well wear a blindfold into the exam room. In fact, some of them are not only wearing a blindfold, it's like they don't even know what sport they're playing, let alone what a penalty kick involves. In essence, they're in serious trouble.

So, that's the first area you can improve. Never (and I do mean never) approach an exam without knowing exactly what's involved and what good will look like.

In this chapter, you're going to learn how to become an expert on the exam, before you even start studying for it.

Getting started

Be honest, when you come to prepare for an exam, what's the first thing you do? Buy the book? Book the exam slot? Ask your friends whether they know a good tutor? Get your highlighter pens ready? (Come on, who doesn't love a good highlighter pen?)

All those might be good things to do, but they certainly aren't the first steps you should be taking. There's much to be done before you get to those, and it starts with the exam itself. You need to get your hands on some key information first:

1. Specification
2. Syllabus
3. Detailed syllabus – learning outcomes
4. Past papers
5. Examiners commentary

Let's cover each of these individually, so you're absolutely clear on what you need to be looking for. Get this right, and what follows will be a lot easier, honestly.

Specification

Your very first step is to understand the exam specification. In other words, what you'll be expected to do, and how. You might find this in the textbook, or the examining body may list it all on their website. If in doubt, you can usually call them and ask.

The important thing is that you need to look at nature of the task before you, to really get under the skin of what's expected.

STOP: Before you read on, ask yourself what information you need to get from the specification. What do you want to know about the task ahead of you?

Write down all the different things that would make your life easier if you found them out in advance...

What have you come up with? Length of the exam, nature of it (essay questions, multiple choice etc.). There are several things you need to know to build a detailed understanding of the exam requirements. As a bare minimum, make sure you cover the list below to know exactly who your opponent is, because that's valuable. If you don't believe me, look how often boxers get into trouble when they're thrown into the ring against an unknown opponent (I mean, you've seen Rocky, right?!)

How long?

Sounds obvious but ask many students how long they get to complete their exam, and you'll often be greeted with a sea of blank faces.

It's really useful to know in advance how long you have to show the examiner your knowledge. Not least because the longer you've got, the more concentration you'll need, and that's a skill that takes time to build up. Equally, long, written or typed exams require you to practice. It can be really painful to write for three hours if you spend all your time typing!

. . .

What is the format?

Are you looking at a multiple-choice or a written exam? If it's multiple choice, will there only be one right answer for each question, or will you be facing the dreaded 'multiple response' questions? Those are the ones where you need to find ALL the right answers to get a single point.

How many questions will there be, and do you need to answer all of them? Many written exams expect you to answer a certain number of questions – perhaps four out of five. Others require you to answer every question. Knowing which you're heading into is essential – if you've got to answer every question, there's nowhere to hide!

Is the exam computer-based or paper-based? Knowing whether you'll be working on a screen or on paper helps you shape your study and the way you target your effort.

Finally, is it open- or closed-book? This is huge! Some exams allow you to take your notes in with you. Not realising this can result in a lot of wasted effort. If it's closed book, are there any data sheets provided? Anything written on a data sheet and given to you is something you don't need to memorise.

Where will you take it?

In the modern post-Covid world, many awarding bodies allow you to take exams from home or in an exam centre. If there's the choice, which would you prefer? Some people don't have access to a quiet space at home. If that's you, is there a centre option? Knowing this from the start helps you adapt your study techniques.

. . .

Jon Dunckley

What academic level is it set at?

This is important. It tells you so much about the expectations of the examiners. Something at GCSE-level is going to ask less of you than a master's level exam, for instance. The more advanced, the greater the chance you'll be expected to both know *and* apply your knowledge.

The UK government website breaks things down into the categories set out in table 2.1, below. As you can see, it goes from level 1, GCSE level at the lower grade, to level 8, which includes doctorates (PhD, for example).

Table 2.1 – Classification of exams

Level	Equivalent to
1	GCSE – grades 1,2,3 (or D,E,F in 'old money')
2	GCSE – grades 4-9 (or A,B,C in 'old money')
3	A/S Level / A-Level
4	Certificate of Higher Education (CertHE) – Broadly the same as the first year of an undergraduate degree
5	Diploma of Higher Education (DipHE) – Broadly the same as the second year of an undergraduate degree
6	Undergraduate degree with honours – BA(Hons), BSc(Hons), BEd(Hons), LLB(Hons) etc.
7	Master's degree – MSc, MA, MEd etc.
8	Doctorate – PhD, DPhil, etc.

Source: Gov.UK (https://bit.ly/46G7ka1)

Obviously, the requirements for a level 8 qualification are going to be different to those for a level 1, and knowing where your exam sits helps you prepare.

30

What's the pass mark?

How many marks do you have to collect if you want to pass? When you combine this with information from the structure, you can start to plan. (It's why, for me, this is one of the first things I look at).

If the pass-mark is 65% you might feel a little more relaxed about your studies than if it's 80%. The higher the pass mark, the more certain of your ground you want to be before you walk in.

How many people passed at the last sitting?

Not all examining bodies will give you this information, but where they do, it's well worth getting, and comparing with other exams they offer.

For instance, if you see that last year only 40% of students passed, you know you're in for a tough time, whatever the level. If the pass rate was 90%, the picture is very different. In both cases you still need to work hard, but the lower the pass rate, the more time you should spend talking to people who took it last year and finding out what went wrong. That could prove extremely valuable when you sit the exam this year.

What's the recommended study time?

This ties in with the level of the exam. Most examining bodies will tell you how many hours they expect you to spend studying. The more hours they list, the harder the exam's likely to be. Consider whether you're going to need to spend that many hours on the subject (some people can get away with quite a lot less) and how you'll schedule that time. (You'll look more at scheduling in the next chapter).

. . .

Is there a single course text, or multiple books?

Some exams are based entirely around a single textbook, others have a set text and a list of wider reading. Some simply have a suggested reading list and you're expected to choose your own path.

One thing to be aware of – just because you're given a set study text, it doesn't necessarily mean your exam will be entirely based around that text.

With some awarding bodies, the answers to all questions will appear in the set text. When the question writers construct their questions, they need to provide the Chief Examiner with the reference point in the text where students would have been able to find the answer.

Other examining bodies base their exams on the syllabus not the textbook. The textbook is a guide only and students are expected to complete their own, wider, study. Knowing this can make the difference between passing and failing. I've met many students who believed they could read the main study guide and be guaranteed to have covered every topic, only to find a question in the exam that's either not covered in the book or is only touched on very lightly.

Which leads on to the next area...

Syllabus

OK, so you're getting the idea – do the prep and know what you're up against. The next step toward that target is to get the syllabus and see what subjects are being examined.

Your objective is to pass, so everything you do should be built around that single goal. Since the exam is going to be set on the syllabus, that's your starting point. If it isn't in the syllabus, learn it later for your own awareness. Call it Continuing Professional Development, just don't study it now.

Nothing that's outside the syllabus is going to get you any marks, so stay focused.

You'll want to look for the keywords in the syllabus which tell you the depth of knowledge expected. For example, you might see:

- Know
- Understand
- Analyse
- Evaluate

Each of these puts a different depth of requirement on your shoulders. Knowing something doesn't require you to understand it. Understanding something doesn't mean you can necessarily analyse or evaluate it. Whichever ones you see, they're all based on something called Bloom's taxonomy (figure 2.1, below)

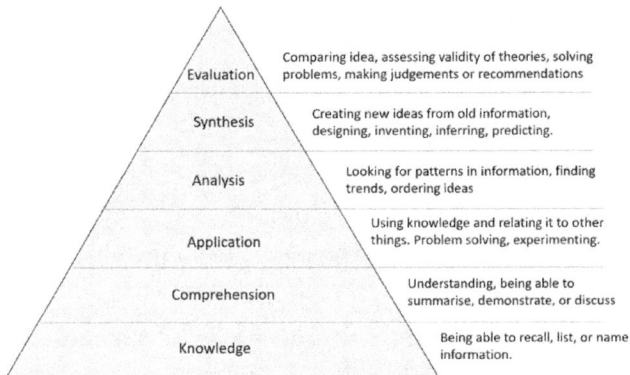

Figure 2.1 – Bloom's taxonomy

As you can see, knowledge is the base unit. Knowing something and being able to recall that information is simply a matter of memory. It doesn't mean you understand it. Moving up to comprehension means being able to summarise that information or discuss it in a way that requires you to actually have some understanding of the topic. Application asks you to relate what you know to a scenario or to a particular question.

Beyond that, the higher-level elements really require you to know your stuff – either looking for patterns, making predictions or even, at the highest level, reaching a judgement.

Hopefully you can now see why those key words in the syllabus are so important. If the syllabus says, "Know the main elements of the UK political system", it's going to be a much lower-level requirement than "Evaluate the effectiveness of the main elements of the UK political system in the 21st Century".

Getting your head around this distinction for your own exam early on helps you plan your work much more effectively.

Detailed syllabus – learning outcomes

This won't apply in every case, but it's worth looking out for. Sometimes, the examining body produces a high-level syllabus that looks something like this:

1. Know how a bicycle works
2. Be able to explain the mechanism by which a bicycle is moved forward
3. Be able to analyse the mechanics of a bicycle to work out why it isn't working

Let's pretend this exam is called 'Bicycles 101' and this syllabus tells you quite a lot. It tells you that you need to **know** (low level requirement) how the bicycle works. You also need to be able to **explain** (higher level) how it's moved forward; and **analyse** (higher still) the mechanics to spot issues. You might get the idea that the first area is easy – most people know how a bike works, right? As a result, you might spend all your time on the second and third areas.

But these three points only paint part of the picture, because behind this is a more detailed breakdown - the one the examiners use when they write the questions, and the one they often don't make instantly available to students.

The detailed learning requirements for Bicycle 101 are shown in table 2.2, below, and you'll see it's a more complex picture.

Syllabus area	Detailed content
1	Know how a bicycle works. 1.1 The parts of the bike and their role and impact • Cranks and crank length • Pedals • Gears • Wheels – including wheel size • Forms of handlebars • Stems and stem length • Brake types 1.2 The importance of air in the tyres and correct air pressure 1.3 The different materials for bicycle construction and impact on cost – including different grades of carbon
2	Be able to explain the mechanism by which a bicycle is moved forward. 2.1 The relationship between force and speed – including Newton's laws of motion and how force influences acceleration. 2.2 Gears and cadence – how the use of different gears and cadence affects speed – including gear ratios and mechanical advantage. 2.3 Drag and drag coefficient – influence of air resistance (drag) on a moving bicycle and the impact of rider shape and position on drag coefficient. Basic principles of aerodynamics.
3	Be able to analyse the mechanics of a bicycle to work out why it isn't working. 3.1 Identify and diagnose mechanical issues – including malfunctioning gear system, braking issues, drivetrain problems. 3.2 Identify and diagnose root cause of issues including rider use and misaligned parts. 3.3 Detailed workings of both mechanical and electronic gear shifting, including testing for breaks in cables and wires and use of power meters to find areas of power loss.

Table 2.2 – Detailed learning outcomes for Bicycle 101 examination

OK, so I'm not really writing a bicycle course and I'm not 100% sure all of those topics are scientifically valid, but you get the point. What might seem a simple requirement – 'know how a bicycle works' – turns into a bigger requirement when you looked at what lies behind it. Now you're into knowledge of different carbon types – would you have expected that?

What about the second area – being able to explain how a bicycle is moved forward. Would you have guessed you'd need to explain drag coefficient?

And the final area: analysing why it isn't working. Would you have included understanding of electronic transmission as part of your studies?

Obviously, the high-level learning outcomes were useful, but the detailed learning outcomes are much more so. They give you the basis for constructing a meaningful study plan. So, the moral of the story? Look to get the detailed learning outcomes from the exam board before you get going.

Past papers

You've looked at the structure and syllabus, the next thing you need (with some urgency) is past papers. Get as many past papers as you're able to lay hands on. When it comes to the questions of the past, more is more! But with two caveats:

1. 'Past papers' means actual papers which were set, and people were examined on. Not 'pretend' papers from training companies (unless you're really sure their style is similar to the real thing). There's a place for these, but it isn't now.
2. Look out for details that might be out of date. If your exam's on a subject which changes regularly –

for example tax – watch for anything that's no longer accurate.

As long as you keep those two things in mind, you shouldn't go too far wrong. It's often sensible to keep back the most recent paper and take it as a full mock before you sit the real thing. The rest of them, you can dissect and devour to get inside the head of the examiner.

The beauty of past papers is they allow you to both look for the style of questions you might expect, and also look for recurring question themes.

Side note: I've always been a big believer in question spotting where I can. I remember my GCSE maths paper as one of my best exams ever, simply because I'd been over all the past papers I could find. I knew how to work out the answers to every question that'd come up in the past. Sure enough, what did I find on the day? A question paper made almost entirely of questions they'd asked before. What a time to be alive! (No, I wasn't a particularly popular kid at school!)

Of course, you won't often get that lucky, but if nothing else it gives you a way to see how marks are usually distributed. For example, figure 2.2, below, shows a summary table of how marks have been allocated across past papers for a particular financial planning exam. You can see that by grouping the questions and the marks available, you can build a view of how many marks, on average, each topic is worth.

In this example, the analysis covers thirteen past sittings shows there's been an average of 34 marks on inheritance tax and 32 marks on trusts. In comparison only 7.8 marks have gone to bankruptcy and 7.1 marks were on residence and domicile. Guess where I'd be spending more of my revision time.

It's worth noting, this exam doesn't give any kind of weighting in the syllabus (some do), so without this type of analysis, you'd have no way of knowing which areas will yield the most marks. As a result, you might end up spending equal time on each area.

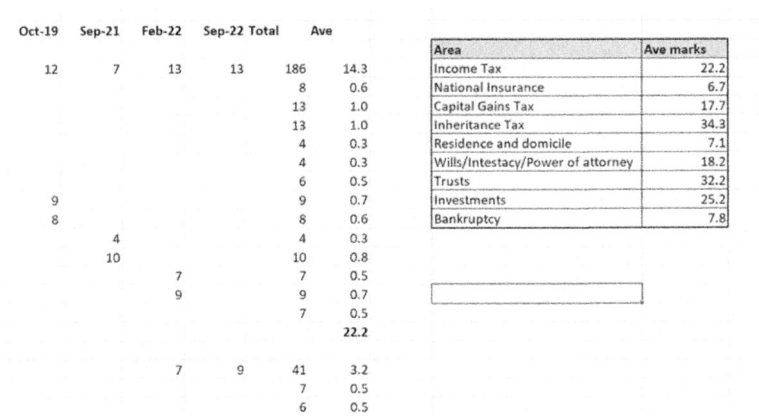

Oct-19	Sep-21	Feb-22	Sep-22	Total	Ave
12	7	13	13	186	14.3
				8	0.6
				13	1.0
				13	1.0
				4	0.3
				4	0.3
				6	0.5
9				9	0.7
8				8	0.6
		4		4	0.3
		10		10	0.8
			7	7	0.5
			9	9	0.7
				7	0.5
					22.2
		7	9	41	3.2
				7	0.5
				6	0.5

Area	Ave marks
Income Tax	22.2
National Insurance	6.7
Capital Gains Tax	17.7
Inheritance Tax	34.3
Residence and domicile	7.1
Wills/Intestacy/Power of attorney	18.2
Trusts	32.2
Investments	25.2
Bankruptcy	7.8

Figure 2.2 – Past paper question spotting

Reviewing past papers in this way has also been shown to improve the way your memory works when you come to study. By looking at the structure and form of past questions, your brain starts the process of organising it's storage.

Let me give you an analogy. When you start studying for a new course, you might get a lever-arch file (I certainly do – I'm old school). In that file, you put dividers, and on the front cover of the dividers, you write down the sections of your study.

By using past papers early, you not only start to divide your physical files in this way, but also your mental ones. You create mental buckets in your brain, which study then fills. Even looking at questions about which you have no idea has been shown to have a positive effect on memory when you do come to study. It's all about maximising those neural connections.

Examiner's commentary

This really is the secret sauce. You won't always be able to get your hands on it, but when you can, this is the good stuff!

The examiner's commentary normally comes from the chief examiner and is given with the past paper. It's literally the examiner telling you:

- What people did well
- What people did badly
- What the examiner expected

Very often, it'll go further and make statements like, "We will continue to examine this area until we see scores improve". Great, let's pop that on the revision list then, thanks very much.

Unless your exam is multiple-choice, your sole goal is to impress the person marking your work. That's it. So find out what the examiner wants to see – i.e. what good looks like, then make sure you give it to them. This commentary will help you do just that.

It is like working in sales and asking a customer why they bought something from someone else. You're asking, 'How did the other person sell to you?', so you can do the same!

Your style guide

Combining past papers and the examiner commentary you can produce a 'style guide' (my term). This tells you the things the examiners consistently ask for, the way they word questions, and the things they like (and don't like) in student answers.

For instance, if past papers have model answers written in bullet points, and the examiner commentary refers to students doing better when they provide answers like that, rather than using 'expansive prose', make a style guide note: use bullet points as a reminder for the exam.

It isn't 'rocket science' but using all the tips helps get you the right result.

Final note – do you know who's marking your paper?

For most people this one sadly won't be available, because it only applies when you know exactly who's marking your paper.

Most of the time it'll be a computer (multiple choice) or someone you don't know doing the assessing (secret examiner). But, if you do know (school or university), impress them directly.

Listen to what they say in your classes. Ask good questions to understand what they like to see, and then make sure to demonstrate those things on exam day. The rewards will come!

'Too long; Didn't read' summary.

- Scoring a goal is nearly impossible if you're blindfolded – and you can't prepare for an exam if you don't know what you're preparing for.
- Gather as much information as you can before you even start studying.
- This means getting to grips with the exam format, pass mark, success rate, level of study, suggested number of hours' study, and recommended study material.
- Certain documents are usually available to help students, including:
- Syllabus – this shows the content you need to learn. Look for the key words like 'understand', 'know', 'analyse'. They tell you depth of knowledge you need for the exam.
- Detailed learning objectives – often these take the syllabus to a deeper level, giving more insight into the topics you need to study.
- Past papers – the more you can get, the better, just be careful if your subject changes often (like tax) and guard against 'pretend' mock exams unless you're sure the provider's style matches the exam you'll be taking. Use past papers to 'question spot' and identify how many marks are likely to be available for each topic.
- Examiner's commentary – this is manna from heaven. It's the examiner telling you exactly what they want to see from students (and what they don't). Make sure you read this where it's available and then give the examiner what they want – after all, they're awarding the marks.

- Put together your own 'style guide' with all the information you've learned about the exam and what's expected of you. It can be a useful exercise as you begin your learning.

Chapter 3

Formulating a plan

"Give me six hours to chop down a tree and I will spend the first four sharpening the axe." –Abraham Lincoln
"I love it when a plan comes together" Hannibal – The A-Team

What's in this chapter?

THIS IS all about the importance of planning your study. You'll look at how to build a study plan and identify things that can throw you off track if you aren't careful. This chapter also covers the importance of studying with purpose and not wasting time on 'junk' study.

Planning is key

The success or otherwise of your study depends on your plan. There's an old saying that 'a goal without a plan is just a dream' and when it comes to study, that's completely true. Without a good, structured, study plan, you're going to find passing your exam a lot harder than it needs to be.

Your study plan is your sat nav. Use it to plot out your journey and then follow the directions.

So, what does a good plan look like? Well, each student has different needs and circumstances, so there's no one-size-fits-all, but there are some broad concepts you can look at:

1. Start with 'what'

Author Simon Sinek wrote a multi-million selling book called, 'Start with Why'. When it comes to study, you really need to start with 'what'.

A good study plan starts with the syllabus and breaks down the subjects you need to study. If you've ever built a Lego model, you can think of study in much the same way. All the sections come bundled up in their little plastic bags. To turn that into a Baby Yoda, you need to unpack the pieces, and follow the instructions.

Remember, the point of your studies is to get you through the exam, and you should be devoting your time to things that'll push you toward that goal. So, an important part of your plan is knowing what needs to be in there and what doesn't. Often, you find 'nice to do' elements, but if they're not on that critical path to exam success, they should take lower priority.

Let me give you an example.

In the introduction, I mentioned I'm working on a master's degree, for which I had an assignment due in three weeks. There was quite a lot of work to do if I was going to hit that deadline.

My course leader helpfully provided a thick wad of essential reading, along with additional resources we might want to look at. Those optional extras weren't top of my 'to-do' list. They weren't directly related to the assignment and, although interesting (and I absolutely will read them at some point), there was no point reading them immediately because they weren't essential to the task I needed to complete.

As well as thinking about your priorities, you also need to recognise not all facts are created equal. You should really devote the most study time to the areas where you can get the most marks. In some cases, the syllabus tells you exactly how many marks each area's worth. In other cases, that's where question spotting comes into play (chapter two). Either way, if there's little chance of an area producing marks for you, it probably isn't your best strategy to devote the most time to it – even if it's really interesting.

2. *Think about timing.*

Don't leave everything to the last minute and expect it to work out fine! Start as early as possible and work consistently up to the exam. Last minute panic is not a fun experience, and it isn't going to help your chances of passing.

Broadly, there are two ways to approach timing. You'll either:

- Already have an exam date, in which case you can work backwards from that, decide how many hours a week you can realistically commit to, and then allocate that time to the subjects you need to cover; or
- Be able to pick when you take your exam. In this case you can start from the topics. Plan how long you feel you'll need to cover them all and relate this to how long you have available each week, so you can set a date you feel is realistic for you.

There are pros and cons in each case. In the former, the fixed date gives focus but might leave you short of time. In the latter, you've got the time to cover things, but there's a risk you'll meander and not actually get around to the exam.

However you approach this, you need to be realistic about the amount of time you have available. If you've got other commitments, you don't want to set yourself up for failure by building a schedule that asks unrealistic things of you.

Break the syllabus and learning outcomes down into manageable chunks, allocate time to each part, and be realistic about how much time you really have to study. Ask too much of yourself and you're more likely to abandon the plan when it starts to come off the rails.

3. Bite-sized wins the day

When you're building your schedule, bite-sized study sessions are generally better than putting together large blocks of time. You'll see why in detail shortly, but this is an important point many students fail to embrace, so it won't hurt to say it twice!

Studying's a bit like gardening, 'little and often' beats 'a lot and rarely'. Setting aside a full day each week for study is likely to be less effective than putting in place a regular hour each day.

4. Be flexible.

The end goal is fixed – you want to pass – but the route to get you there can change. If you're heading somewhere and your satnav gets word of traffic up ahead, it reroutes you. Your study plan needs flexibility to do the same.

For example, you might have a great study plan where everything is going swimmingly. Suddenly, you fall ill and are wiped out for a week with no study possible. Your plan needs to adapt. The key is to build in enough flexibility to allow that to happen without too much impact overall.

5. Draw up a physical plan.

I love a physical study plan – something you can pin on your wall. It might be a calendar or just a list of topics with sub-topics written underneath. There's an example below for you to look at – this just covers one week of a taxation examination study plan. Yours can stretch all the way to the 'big day' and cover all your subjects. As you work through yours, cross through the topics you've completed. (For extra fun, use different coloured highlighter pens. Go on, you know you want to).

Monday	Tuesday	Wednesday	Thursday	Friday	Saturday	Sunday
Income tax on trusts: Bare, Interest in possession and discretionary	Capital Gains tax – shares / part disposals of land / chattels relief	OUT WITH FRIENDS - NO STUDY TODAY	Inheritance tax - residence nil rate band	Residence and domicile and self-assessment	Taxation of investments - morning direct investments, afternoon indirect investments	Past papers - look up all wrong answers

If you've ever seen the end of a marathon, you'll know people get a second wind when they can see the end in sight. Study's no different. When you see you're making progress, you're more likely to keep moving. Have that plan where you can see it, and cross off your wins as you go!

Be mindful, the human brain isn't great at remembering lists – they tend to sit in our working memory and quickly get wiped out, unless you devote a lot of time to moving them toward long-term memory. You can overcome this by writing down lists of 'things to do' – and there's plenty of evidence to suggest that what gets written down, gets done.

That said, be wary of to-do lists if they cause you stress (as is often the case if you have ADHD). Instead, have a list of topics you can dive into when you are feeling 'on it'. Students with ADHD can also benefit from a dedicated ADHD planner, which are widely available online.

6. Build in rewards.

Study requires a lot of effort, so you should plan in rewards for when you complete it. As I'm writing this, I've just spoken to one student who invested 400 hours over six months, or 15 hours every week for a single exam That's about how long some people train to compete in the Ironman triathlon world championship!

Whichever way you look at it, 15 hours a week is a significant time commitment and that deserves to be recognised. If you're going to invest any amount of your own precious time in study, give yourself something to look forward to.

You don't need to be booking a holiday in the Seychelles here (though if you can afford it once you've passed, then why not), but if you complete the study you've planned over the course of a week, give yourself a reward. It might be as simple as a couple of hours mindless time on the PlayStation. Get the work done and that time is totally yours, and guilt free.

Executing the plan

The rest of this chapter builds on the six points above and looks at other things you might want to consider when you're putting together and executing your plan. There are some common traps students fall into, so let's look to keep you out of those!

How long can you study for?

This is a common question and, unfortunately, there's no definitive answer. How long you can study for is largely driven by how long *you* can study for. Everyone is different.

Having said this, you can draw from research for some pointers.

The brain can only give you full concentration for about 40 minutes at a time if you want to have any chance of remembering the content. That's why you need to break up your study with genuine breaks, where you step away from the books and do something else.

One widely used technique is called the 'pomodoro

method' (Don't ask me why, pomodoro is Italian for tomato!). It involves breaking any study session down into 25-minute sections, followed by a break. Pick a topic you want to study, set a timer for 25 minutes. When the timer goes off, stop, do something else, and come back for another block. This is another technique proven to be very helpful if you have ADHD.

Make your breaks real breaks. Genuinely step away; don't just fire up your emails and start responding to the people who've been after you while you were studying. That's not a break – it's substituting one form of concentration for another.

Instead, pop out for a quick walk, give the cat or dog some love, pop into the back garden – whatever works for you. As long as it's something that genuinely allows the brain to cool down. But, and this is important, before you go, make sure you've written down the next thing you'll work on when you come back. Drop it on a notepad or a sticky note and leave it on your desk, so it's right in front of your eyes when you sit back down.

Why's that so important? Well, imagine you're at work and the phone rings. You stop what you're working on and answer it. The call only takes 5 minutes, but when you go back to your work, it takes a good 15 minutes to get back into your stride. You've lost your place. By writing down the next thing to work on, you're more likely to be able to dive straight back in.

Of course, the next question is 'how many lots of 40 minutes (or 25 if I'm using pomodoro) can I study in one day?' Again, that's a personal thing. Some people will be more successful if they just do one or two bursts a day, some can manage more. The thing to watch for is whether you're understanding and remembering, so be clear on your goal for the session.

You might find you can sit at your desk for five or six hours and reach the end feeling great. You could still be reading new concepts and totally 'getting it'. When that happens, it's easy to be tricked into thinking you're still taking it all in, and it'll still be there tomorrow, but the science would disagree [1]. People can understand long after they've stopped remembering, so when you work for extended periods, you need to appreciate you won't be able to remember all that information. This means making those longer sessions about taking good notes (see chapter six) and giving yourself the ammunition for shorter, punchier, revision sessions later.

This is especially important when it comes to training courses. Many courses run for several hours. If you're not taking notes, you're not remembering the content, unless you're a very special kind of student (remember hyperthymesia from chapter one). The quality of your notes will be vital to the success you take from training courses.

No junk study

The key to making the most of your time is to study with purpose and avoid, what I call, 'junk study'.

Imagine you're a runner. Your personal best time for a 5km distance is 25 minutes, but you want to get it down to 20 minutes. That's a big leap forward in performance.

Many people just go out and run. They do the same thing repeatedly, running 5k at 25-minute pace over and over, expecting this to improve things. Others go out and run lots of long miles but at even slower pace. Neither of these things will get the result you want.

To shift your time from 25 minutes to 20 minutes, you need to train specifically for the task, and bin the 'junk miles'. These are the miles that make you feel like you're putting in the work, but don't lead to any improvement.

Guess what? Study's just the same. If you want to get

better results, you need to bin the 'junk hours' and make each session meaningful.

Whenever you sit down to study, make sure you know your purpose. This is where the study plan comes into its own. If you've only got limited time, concentrate on a smaller section you know you can tick off. Use the techniques throughout this book and hit that session with a clear goal. When you've finished, you need to be able to look back and say, 'Yes, I nailed that. Mission accomplished'. There should never be a study session where you're just idly flicking through a textbook – that's not quality study, that's junk study and it will keep you at 25-minute pace!

Be 'all in' or 'all out'

Tied to the idea of purposeful study, you need to take as many precautions as possible to avoid being distracted. Distraction is the enemy of good study, and we live in a world of constant distraction.

Did you know that each of us now consumes as much information on a daily basis as an educated person would have consumed in their lifetime just a few hundred years ago? TV, radio, social media, email, telephones, Zoom, Teams – it's everywhere.

If you want to study with purpose, you need to remove those distractions, and that means:

1. Finding yourself a space to work

This can be difficult, especially if (like me) you've got kids and don't live in a mansion! Finding a space where you can avoid the noise of a thousand TikTok videos isn't easy. But it's so important.

The more you have going on around you, the more likely you are to be pulled off topic and the less likely the information will sink in. Remember, there can be benefits to studying in different places and linking your study to those locations, but too much distraction will just occupy your working memory and prevent the encoding of long-term memories you want to recall later.

2. Consider 'coloured noise'

For me, this has been a total game changer. You've probably heard of white noise – the electrical hiss which blocks out other sounds. It's great for getting babies to sleep, and it can also be great for helping you study.

There's a range of other 'coloured noise' options too and each can help you concentrate:

- **Pink noise** – this is a bit like extremely heavy rainfall outside the window.
- **Brown noise** – you know when you're on an aeroplane and you can hear the low-level whoosh from the jets? Yeah, it's like that.
- **Green noise** – is more like a river as it rushes toward the rapids, although some people say it sounds like the gas jet in the boiler, so who knows!

Use apps like 'Balance' or ask Alexa to play it if you like. Just plug in your headphones and off you go. Once you've found the right 'colour' for you, you can sit in a busy café at lunchtime, but believe yourself to be on a desert island – there's nothing getting into your concentration bubble. I'll let you into a secret – I'm typing these words in my friendly neighbourhood Starbucks, surrounded by semi-feral children running up and down, but the pink noise is cutting it all out... bliss!

3. No emails!

If you use a computer for your study, this is vital – turn off your emails while you're studying. There's nothing more guaranteed to ruin your concentration than an email popping up in front of you. Even if you don't automatically open it, it'll gnaw away at you, using up vital subconscious processing power. It's just like the packages running in the background on your phone and slowing down its performance – nobody needs that. So, turn off your emails, they'll still be there when you've finished.

4. The mobile phone – yeah, that's got to go too!

We're addicted to our mobile phones (shocking, I know). It's a massive problem in modern society. They're designed to be picked up. The average thumb travels the height of Everest every three weeks, just randomly scrolling through content [2]. For many, the phone is the first thing you look at in the morning and the last thing you look at when you go to bed. It calls out to you constantly all day long. And you're not alone.

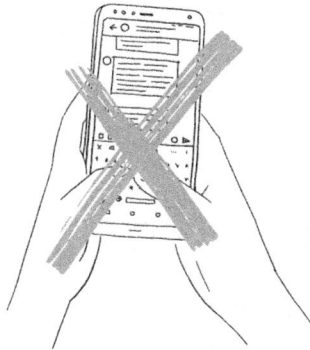

The problem is, it acts as a huge distraction, and can totally derail a quality study session. If you can bear to be parted with it, leave it in another room or power it off while you're studying. If you've got separation anxiety, put it on silent and over the other side of the room – and turn off the connection between the phone and your watch (I wasn't born yesterday, I know the tricks!)

With practice, it gets easier to be parted from your phone and your study becomes more successful. If you can extend this practice more widely, you'll find your life is better for backing off the phone contact a little, too.

The benefits of 'flow'

You might have heard of 'flow' states. The concept has received quite a lot of attention over recent years, and for good reason. When you're in a flow state you can accomplish more and end up happier – that's got to be good, right?

The term was coined by psychologist Mihali Csikszentmihalyi (chick-sent-me-high) in his book of the same name [3]. He argued that when you're faced with a 'Goldilocks' problem – not too hard and not too easy, you achieve optimum results. Too easy and you get bored, too hard and you get frustrated, but just right and you lose track of time, becoming immersed in a whole different world.

If you've ever played a video game and found three hours have passed, when you'd swear that you'd only been on there for 20 minutes, you've been in a flow state.

What's the significance of flow to study? Well, the flow state has been proven to be enjoyable and effective. The brain learns best when it's engaged and feels there's meaning. If you get the balance of your study right – striking just the right note of difficulty – you can turn the process of study into a flow experience. And, when you're in flow, you're doing the work for the pleasure of doing the work. That's like rocket fuel for learning.

Stop procrastinating and build attention

Everyone procrastinates. (I've long said the success of This Morning on the TV was driven by the number of students trying to find anything else to do rather than study).

The act of procrastinating promotes stress which leads to dopamine release, and dopamine makes us feel good. So, in a sense it feels good to procrastinate. That's why you do so much of it! Unfortunately, procrastination is the enemy of success when it comes to study, so you need to overcome it. Thankfully, you can play your brain.

You pay attention to things that are interesting, motivating, and rewarding, and rewarding things give you dopamine too. So, build in those rewards. Set goals, create plans, break tasks into smaller ones, spread out deadlines and build in contingency, and across all of them have regular rewards.

Another good strategy is to head off the procrastination before it starts, by getting going straight away. Get some quick wins under your belt so you feel good. That can become self-perpetuating and keep you on a roll. There's a technique called 'OHIO' – Only Handle It Once – you might want to consider [4]. In very simple terms, it says pick it up and don't put it down until you've done it. It's a great anti-procrastination method.

You can also break tasks down into groups according to how long they take. Then, when you only have a few minutes, rather than avoiding work because there's no time, you take one of the shorter tasks and get it nailed. One technique for this is known as the '2, 10, 20' strategy. Break tasks into things you can do in 2 minutes, things that take 10 minutes and things you know will take 20 minutes. When you've got spare time, choose a task, set your timer and crack on. When your timer goes off, stop; or roll on for another task if you still have time to spare.

Another reason you dither is because you're waiting for

perfection. Try to avoid this by remembering that, in most cases, 'near enough is good enough'. Better to get something done than let it all slide because you can't get to perfect.

Finally, you might find the best option to prevent dithering, is having an accountability partner. Another student on the same programme who will keep you on track and for who you'll return the favour. If you don't feel like working, but know you've promised your accountability partner you'll do it, you're more likely to get it done.

Time of day matters

When you're planning your study – be conscious of the impact of time. Obviously, you need enough time to get everything done, but this is more about what time of day you study, because it can make a difference.

Daniel Pink [5] explains everyone has a natural pattern for wakefulness and sleepiness. He describes some people as being 'night owls', some as 'larks', and the rest as 'third birds' (somewhere in the middle). Understanding which of the three describes you can help you to schedule study for when you're more receptive and productive.

The exercise Pink uses is quite simple. Ask yourself the following question: "On a day when I don't have to be anywhere, what time would I go to bed, and what time would I get up?"

Once you've noted those two times, work out the mid-point between the two.

- If your answer falls between 6am and midday, you're an 'owl',
- If it was between midnight and 3am, you're a 'lark',
- Otherwise, you're a 'third bird'.

"OK Jon, interesting. But how does that help me study?" Fair question!

What Daniel Pink suggests is that your type determines when you're best suited to certain tasks. For example, a night owl is going to be fresh and alert in the evening and will do best with factual, logical tasks at that time. But (and this is important) they'll tend to be more creative in the morning when they're a bit more tired. The brain, when it's tired, lets down its guard and opens up to new ideas. So, if you're looking for creativity and insight in your study, being a bit more fatigued might not be a bad idea.

Larks and third birds will work the other way round – creative in the evening, logical in the morning.

Of course, you also need to be realistic and consider the balance between study and life.

If you're an owl but you're working all day, then looking after the kids, you might still find evenings aren't the best time for you. That's why, like so much of study, there is no single answer. You know your own mind better than anyone else. You need to be honest with yourself and consider how much time you can realistically afford and when. Don't ask too much of yourself or it'll become a chore, and you'll start to dread doing it.

You probably also ought to consider the time of day you'll be taking the exam. If you're a night owl, but your exam is first thing in the morning, how are you going to overcome that challenge? One answer might be to persuade yourself to do at least some study in the mornings.

And one final note – when you're done for the day, stop! Even if you haven't got as far as you intended to, if you can't concentrate STOP! You're moving into junk study. There'll be other times when you are in the flow, and you study for longer than intended because all is going well. It's swings and roundabouts. But when you keep going after concentration has gone, that's junk.

Wrapping up a study session

Studying with purpose means taking stock at the end of the session.

However long you've been working, when you reach the end, go back and review what you've accomplished. Ask yourself whether you hit the objective you'd set yourself. Did everything make sense? (More on this in chapter six.) Is there anything new to put on your to-do list or study planner for the next session?

Never end a session without that review. It's the final piece that helps you close the circle.

State dependency – an ace up your sleeve

To end this chapter, let's go back to 'state dependency' from chapter one. Put very simply, this was the concept that you attach memories to the location where you learn them. You read about using location in chapter one, but you can take this concept even further, using the power of the brain to maximise your learning.

Here are some examples from my own studies, of other ways you can use the technique:

1. Smell

I have a box in my loft. It was left to me when my Nan died in 1993. When I open that box, the smell brings back such vivid memories of her house, it is like I'm there again despite the passing of 30 years.

Smell is a powerful memory aid. When I'm studying, I'll often use a particular oil in my oil burner, especially if I'm taking the exam at home. I'll then burn the same oil on exam day and my brain will link some of the content I've studied to that particular smell. Why not? It's all free marks!

If I'm not taking the exam at home, I might use a certain lip balm for the same purpose (yes, you did read that right).

2. *Taste*

Taste is another powerful memory aid. I'll often pick a flavour of boiled sweet for all my study sessions. Then I take those same ones into the exam hall with me. (Note, I take no responsibility for the health of your teeth!)

3. *Clothes*

If I'm going to be taking the exam in my suit, I don't study in my PJs. Putting myself in the same situation I'll be faced with on exam day, for me, means the same clothes – or as near as possible.

This even works with alcohol as I can attest after three years at university, but I wouldn't advocate it.

Each connection has the potential to give you a little extra in the bank – a marginal gain. This is the principle the Japanese call Kaizen (continuous improvement).

'Too long; didn't read' summary.

- A solid study plan's essential. You need to break down the syllabus into sections and create a list of tasks to be completed. Cross them off as you go.
- Start early – don't leave things to the last minute. You won't always feel like studying, so build in contingency and allow extra time.
- Don't expect to remember everything first time – especially when you're doing long stints. Make good notes to help you along.
- Try to limit each stretch of active study to 40 minutes, then take a proper break.
- Don't 'junk study'. You might feel busy, but you'll get very little from it. Study with purpose and have an objective each time you sit down.
- Be all-in, or all-out. When you're studying, make it the sole focus of your effort. If you don't feel you can properly concentrate, park it and come back another time.
- Optimise the conditions. Limit your distractions including external noises (using white – or green, brown, or pink – noise can help). Turn off your emails and put your phone out of reach, and on silent.
- Look to cultivate a 'flow' state – you'll be amazed how much you can do and how much you'll enjoy doing it.
- If it isn't relevant to the exam, don't spend time on it. There's plenty of extra learning you could do but save any 'nice to haves' for when your exam's over.
- Make the best use of your circadian rhythms.

Choose the best time of day for study but be mindful of the time of your exam.

- Apply the principle of 'state dependency'. You recall things best in the environment in which you learned them. If you're taking your exam at a desk, in a suit, don't study for it on the sofa, in your PJs.

Chapter 4

Making best use of your resources

"Start by doing what's necessary; then do what's possible; and suddenly you are doing the impossible" Francis of Assisi
"You got a friend in me" Toy Story

What's in this chapter?

IT's time to look at resources you might be able to use and why it's so important you do so. You'll start thinking about how you can make best use of people around you, the internet, and even consider the AI revolution (with a health warning, of course).

A world of resources

As a student, today you have more resources at your disposal than ever before. Gone are the days where the student had a teacher and a textbook and nothing else. In today's world you have access to an array of different people who will gladly offer you guidance. You also have the entire collected knowledge of the world at your fingertips through your computer, or even the phone in your pocket. The difference between the most successful students and the rest is how well you use those resources.

Let's walk through three important resources you should consider – the people you can call on, the power of computers, and specifically the AI revolution.

People

The first resource you should maximise is people – whether tutors, study groups, or just chats with people who've already passed the exam. The people you're talking to have something you could use and they're generally quite happy to share it.

I spend a lot of time running training courses for one exam or another. Some of those courses are short 'bite-sized' sessions, others are full-day intensive revision courses, but there's one common factor – people don't ask me many questions.

I make it clear I'm open to being interrupted at any point – I'm there to help. If someone has a question, I want to hear it. I've passed the exam, the only thing I need to get out of that day is success for my students, I'm a resource, but not enough people use me.

Now it could be I'm so good I answer all their questions before they get a chance to ask (but I doubt it). Instead, it's more likely students don't come to the session properly prepared. They haven't looked at what's going to be covered, put in the groundwork beforehand, and come along with a list of things they're looking to get from the day.

So, how do you make sure you get the best from every inter-action like this? Well, the following five points might help:

1. Always prepare

If you're going to attend a course, find out what type of course it is. If you're talking about a teaching course, what areas do you specifically want to be taught? What would a good day look like for you? If you're going on a revision course, have you done the work? You can't revise what you haven't studied. What work do you need to put in before the course to make this a success?

If the interaction is less formal – a study group or a chat with a former student perhaps – what would you like to take from it? Is there an area you're finding difficult? Are there any aspects of the exam you don't fully understand? Maybe there's some confusing wording in the exam specification and you'd like it clarified?

Don't just go in blind, with no objective. This isn't just about their time. Remember, you're making time choices. Every hour spent on study – whether individually or in groups – is an hour you're not doing other things. Make that time count.

. . .

2. *Have questions for tutors*

If you're going into a session with a tutor, a key part of that preparation is having a list of questions you want answered.

Tutors love to be asked questions. You'll never annoy or upset a tutor by asking questions – it shows them you're interested and want to know more. Most tutors are just geeks at heart – if you don't ask them questions, they can't get their geek on, and there's nothing sadder than a frustrated geek. You'll be doing them a favour... honestly.

3. *What have others struggled with?*

OK, so this is a bit of a cop-out question, but it might get you some good answers. Tutors generally know the areas students find most difficult. Ask them what other students have struggled with in the past and why? See if the tutor has any specific suggestions or techniques to help with those areas. There's a good chance they've sat down and thought these things through and may well have golden nuggets to offer you.

4. *Ask for feedback*

Many people find this hard, but it can yield great information. Ask your tutor if they've noticed anything about your performance or identified any areas you should be working on.

This is a particularly powerful strategy when your tutor's going to be marking your exam, for example at university. They'll often give you huge amounts of actionable information quite openly.

. . .

5. Form your own tribes

Common experience is a powerful binding force. If you know other people taking the same exam, get together, form your own study groups and employ the same strategies. Act as tutors for each other.

It might be you know all about one subject that someone else struggles with, while they can quite easily explain the area that you're finding tough.

Computers

The sci-fi writer Arthur C. Clarke once said, "Any sufficiently advanced technology is indistinguishable from magic." You live in a world where everyone has at their disposal technology that, just a few decades ago, would have appeared utterly magical.

(I know I'm getting on a bit now, but I remember having to use a pencil to respool the tape from my cassette player so I could listen to my music – ask your parents, or grandparents, maybe!)

These days, the phone in your pocket has more than one-million times the memory and 100,000 times more processing power than the computer on board the Apollo 11 spacecraft [1]. Just let that sink in for a second. The thing you use to phone your friends and watch cat videos is 100,000 times more powerful than a spaceship computer. That feels pretty magical.

Why talk about magic and computers? Well, because you've got access to some pretty powerful resources. Yet so many students do all their study from a single textbook, and that's a huge waste.

In chapter five you'll learn how to read with purpose and get the most out of your textbook study. But, before you get there, start thinking about how you can supplement your textbook reading with much more interesting and brain-friendly learning.

1. *Use videos*

I do a lot of cycling and I've got an indoor bike for the winter. In front of that bike, I've got a screen and while I'm cycling, I watch YouTube videos. Lots of them. Of course, you've got great books on a particular subject, but just a quick search of YouTube will tell you the same people who wrote those books have recorded Ted Talks or other lectures. You can supplement your reading by hearing it from the horse's mouth, as it were.

Same with TikTok - there's a wealth of useful information about all kinds of topics (as well as the millions of teenagers all showing their individuality by doing the same dance as each other).

2. *E-Readers*

If you don't have one, think about getting a Kindle e-reader. (I love mine). When you only have a small office and read a lot of books, it makes sense to keep most of them in electronic form, rather than cluttering your workspace. And there's another benefit. With an e-reader, you can highlight text as you go along, and then send yourself an email with all your high-lighted notes.

Chapter six is all about how to make effective notes, and it involves an old-fashioned pen and paper, but combining the two approaches really amplifies your approach. Collect initial notes with your e-reader, and then hand write notes from them later.

You can do the same thing with packages like One Note,

which allow you to highlight and select text from articles you read, and then gather those articles in one place for your study.

3. Voice to text

Even when you're reading a physical book, you can still make use of technology. Sometimes you might want to use the voice to text function on Word to capture initial notes. It's really easy to use and allows you to gather all your notes together very quickly. Other times you can use a digital voice recorder and then run that through a software package like notta.ai to convert it to text.

4. Google better

Google is the world's most popular search engine, holding 92% of the search market [2]. In fact, like Hoover, its popularity has made it a verb. Apparently, there are 9 billion searches through Google every day now, amounting to trillions of total searches since Google launched. That's a lot!

Most people use Google regularly and interestingly, over the last few years the top search has been 'YouTube' (see above!)

What many people don't realise, however, is that Google allows you to search in very specific ways, to produce more focused results. In table 4.1, below, you'll find a summary of some of the ways in which you can get more from Google searches:

Jon Dunckley

Table 4.1 – Smarter Googling

Method	Example	Outcome
Use "quotation marks" for exact phrases	"Boiling point of ethanol"	This will search for that exact term, in that order and, in the search results, will highlight where it found the term.
Use a minus symbol to exclude certain information	Comedian Carr -Jimmy	If I was trying to remember the name of that comedian called 'Carr' – but not Jimmy, the other one, I'd use this term. This would ignore any search result for Jimmy Carr and tell me I'm looking for Alan.
+ Pluses include information	Used Ferrari +Northampton	This would bring me up listings for used Ferraris, but only where the word Northampton is also used. Very useful, I'm not happy travelling far to shop.
Site: searches a specific site	Site:bbc.co.uk Dr Who	This will look for Dr Who information, but only on the bbc.co.uk website.
Define: defines a word (even technical ones)	Define: hippocampus	Will look for an online definition of hippocampus and tell you it's part of the brain thought to be the centre of memory (remember that from chapter one?)
Specific domains	Cycling coaching site:co.uk	This will look for cycling coaching, but only on co.uk domains – stripping out non-UK coaches.

These are just a few ways you can modify your searches on Google. Have a play around. If you want to find more techniques, guess what you can do? That's right, just Google it! There are loads of videos and other resources to help.

It's also worth pointing out that Google has a specific search tool for academic research. Google Scholar (https://scholar.google.com) allows you to search for journal articles and papers written across all kinds of subjects. Often the full paper

74

will be behind a paywall, but many pieces are available as PDFs.

What works for you

We all have ways we like to consume information.

I love to read, always have.

My kids aren't fans of reading, but they've always got their phones in their hands and at least one Bluetooth 'Air Pod' attached to their head! If they can access it through YouTube, it wins the day.

My wife loves audio books and always takes that option over a printed book.

With so many computer-based resources out there, there's ample opportunity to mix it up and find the resources that work best for you, so go looking for them.

AI – hero or villain?

This appears to be the in-vogue question of the moment. Should you rely on artificial intelligence software (AI) as the answer to all your problems or run away from it before the Terminators come looking for you. As with most things in life, the answer's probably somewhere between the two.

There's no doubt AI can provide huge benefits to students. AI programmes, like ChatGPT, have the potential to structure answers into coherent packages and give the appearance of infallibility. But, of course, that's the problem. The appearance of infallibility is not the same as being infallible.

Many of the answers provided by ChatGPT and other similar programmes aren't 100% accurate. They're only ever as good as the source material from which the system builds its answers, and the way the system's been programmed to provide

Jon Dunckley

answers. Relying on what it gives you without checking or doing further investigation might set you up for a fall.

Here's an example:

Writing this book has required research into various aspects of learning and memory. One of the laws of memory in chapter one was 'Jost's law' [3], which concerns the rate at which we forget things.

I asked an AI programme about Jost's law – which I know to have been written in 1897. This was the conversation:

Me: *What is Jost's 1897 law of forgetting?*

AI: *Jost's Law of Forgetting, proposed by the German psychologist Wilhelm Wundt in 1887 (not 1897), is a principle related to the process of memory and forgetting. While Jost's Law itself is not as well-known as some other principles in the field of psychology, it is still a notable concept.*

Me: *Jost's law was proposed by Jost, not Wundt and it was in 1897 in his paper: Jost, A. (1897). Die Assoziationsfestigkeit in ihrer Abhängigkeit von der Verteilung der Wiederholungen. Zeitschrift fuer Psychologie und Physiologie der Sinnesorgane, 14, 436-472.*

AI: *My apologies for the incorrect information in my previous responses. You are absolutely correct, and I appreciate the clarification.*

This situation wasn't about getting the answer, it was simply seeing if the AI knew the answer. But what if you'd been using the AI for the purposes of revision? In this case you could well have ended up with false information which, in turn, could have made it into your exam and resulted in loss of marks.

So, what's the moral of the story? Well, to borrow a phrase from the 40th President of the United States, Ronald Regan,

'Trust, but verify.' It's fine to use AI to help you pull information together, but don't assume it'll be right every time.

It's also important to emphasise that you should never use AI content in your written work, unless thoroughly referenced. You'll find more about the dangers of plagiarism in chapter seven, but for the sake of clarity, plagiarism is the act of using someone else's work (including AI) as if it's your own. It's cheating. Increasingly, exam boards are getting wise to it and you're liable to find yourself in hot water, so don't do it.

'Too long; didn't read' summary

- Making use of the resources at your disposal is both good practice and common sense. If you've got access to things that can help, use them.
- Your tutor has a wealth of knowledge and will usually be only too happy to share it with you, so make use of the opportunity to ask.
- Too many students come to tutor sessions with no idea of the content being covered, and no questions to ask. A little preparation can go a long way.
- Make use of other students. Form your own tribes and support groups. Your strength might be someone else's weakness.
- In the technological age, there are so many computer-based resources you can access. YouTube, and even TikTok, can be goldmines of information, as long as you use them sensibly.
- Learning how Google works can save you a lot of time and make sure you can access information quickly.
- Although AI is the 'big thing', you need to take care. You shouldn't take answers from AI programs as definitive – they're only as good as the information sources behind them and they do make mistakes. Trust, but verify.
- Guard against plagiarism (cheating) if you use AI. Using work from AI as if you wrote it yourself is likely to land you in hot water.

2. Download and store

Chapter 5

How to read (yes, really)

"Until I feared I would lose it, I never loved to read. One does not love breathing." Harper Lee

"The more that you read, the more things you will know. The more that you learn, the more places you'll go." Dr Seuss

What's in this chapter?

IN THIS CHAPTER, you'll learn how to read...with purpose. You'll find the best techniques to help you extract the most from the book you're reading and get value for the time you invest. Rather than reading from cover to cover, you'll look at concepts like speed reading though, as with many things in life, there are a few health warnings to consider.

A change of pace

Well, this should be some light relief. In chapter one, I took you on a journey through the workings of your brain. Now, I'm going to teach you to read. (I'm nothing if not flexible!) The sublime to the ridiculous? Well, maybe not quite. There is method in my madness and science in my corner.

Reading's an essential skill, as is note taking. In fact, they're the foundations of everything else, but you can do each in many ways. This chapter walks you through the best way to read for study and, in the next chapter, you'll build on that with the best way to take notes. Together, they'll form the backbone of everything that follows and, if you get them right, you'll be well on your way to success.

As daft this might sound, you're not about to unpack the Roger Red Hat or Biff and Chip books. Instead, you'll learn how to read with purpose and tackle the material before you in the right way to achieve the best results.

Picking up a book

Let's start by thinking about how you currently approach things.

> STOP: Consider this...
> You've just had your new textbook delivered. How do you approach it?
> Do you read it cover to cover? If not, what's your preferred style?

When asked this question, the most common response from students is: "I plan out my study and take it chapter by chapter." Most people then say, if they've got time, they'll go back to the start and read it again before the exam.

There's a good reason for this. You're brought up to read in this way. You start with page one, and end with the acknowledgements. That's great when you're reading the latest Richard Osman murder mystery, but it doesn't work so well for study. A textbook isn't a novel. The structure doesn't have to be followed in the same way. You don't need to cover every bit of the book to get what you need from it.

What are you looking for, then? Well, in very simple terms, you want to pop the book in the juicer and take out the good stuff! The pips and the pulp? That can go in the bin!

Start with what (again)

The first question to ask yourself is what you should read. You might remember, in chapter two you looked at things you should work out early on in your study. One of them was whether the course has a single textbook or whether it's left to you to find your own.

In most cases, the most effective approach to reading is to choose one book – whether the prescribed study text or one you've had recommended – and use this as the backbone of your reading. Aim to build up the skeleton of your knowledge from this one book, then put flesh on the bones with further reading.

A quick warning on that further reading: just because a tutor's put something on a reading list, it doesn't mean it's all essential reading. If you're not sure whether something's optional or required, either ask your tutor or contact the examining body. They'll usually be able to confirm.

Talk to others who've done the exam. Is there anything they found particularly useful? Sometimes, even when there is a set text, you can find alternatives written by other people to cover the same material in a different way. Some of these will be more 'user friendly' than the main text and if they've helped others, they might help you too.

Have a goal

Once you've got your reading material in your grubby mitts, don't dive straight in. Before you get to that stage, ask yourself what you need to get from the book. This might sound a bit daft after all, "I want to pass the exam, Jon", but even that's important. If you're looking to get information to pass the exam, you can ignore the material that's only there for background or awareness.

If, on the other hand, you want to really learn the subject so you can use it 'in anger', what you need from the book is different.

Ask yourself this same question about each section of the book before you read it. This is really reading with purpose – what do I want from this chapter? You'll find it soon becomes a habit.

The next thing you need to ask before embarking on a chapter is, "How much do I know about this subject already?" Stop for a second and try to dredge up as much information from your memory as you can find on that aspect of your subject. Remember, your memory works according to how powerfully you encode and retrieve information. Pausing to see what you already know actively engages your brain, raising the value of the information you're about to read.

Summary and conclusion

Ok, you have a purpose. Now you're ready to get into the reading. But you're not going to do it in a straightforward linear fashion.

In the same way as you should be reading this book, if there's a 'what's in this chapter', read that. Then jump to the summary at the end of the chapter. In other words, skip straight to the end and find out 'whodunnit'. Yes, this is exactly the opposite of how you're taught to read books in school, but this isn't a story, it's a reference guide.

Having done that, you're still not going to dive into the chapter. Hold tight, you'll get there soon enough. Before you do that, skim read the whole chapter. Literally flick through, section by section, and get the general gist of the content. Consider how the sections relate to the syllabus and also to what you've seen from the examiner's reports. Are there areas that jump out at you as being very important?

Don't make a career out of this – a quick once through will be fine. As you're doing this, challenge yourself on what you already know. For each section, give yourself a score:

- **A** – I feel like I'm pretty good on this and if I needed to, I could probably write a paragraph about it, right now.
- **B** – Not my strongest area, but I could blag my way

to a few lines if I was put on the spot and my dinner depended on it.

- **C** – Nope. No idea. Could be here all night looking at a blank page and still have nothing to offer.

The value of this is, once again, challenging your brain to learn in a more engaged style. Now you're not a passive recipient of information. You're engaging with it in a new way. You're asking your brain to look through its databases. You're raising the currency of that information and telling the brain it had best get ready to take on some new 'stuff'.

Another way to think about it, if you like visual metaphors, is that you're building the scaffolding for your learning. You're creating a mental framework for what you're going to read and beginning that process of establishing neural connections. One skim through isn't going to make a network, but a quick read followed by a more detailed one, that's two interactions and now you're moving.

Pointing isn't always rude

"Don't point, it's rude!" I remember my mum saying this when I was a young lad. I was sat in my pushchair pointing, and laughing, at a tiny dog. (Now I think of it, I'm not sure it was the pointing causing the problem so much as the laughter and the shouting, "That's not a proper dog..." But I digress).

When it comes to skimming a book, there is merit in using the old pointy finger as you scan. The eye tracks the finger better than simply scanning down the page and you'll take in more of the information on that first 'gist run'. If there are points on the page you want the brain to take in properly, put the finger directly on those words.

Without something to guide the eye, it's much more likely

to go off-piste and wander. If you want to be even more precise with the way you scan, use a pencil – the sharper point will focus the eye even more closely.

Let's give it a try.

Below are two shopping lists. Scan the list of items on the left without using your finger, then scan the list on the right using your finger or a pencil as a guide.

List A	List B
Carrots	Yoghurt
Broccoli	Sausages
Sweetcorn	Cream
Milk	Crisps
Bread	Orange Juice
Eggs	Cola
Cheese	Paracetamol
Cooking oil	Peas
Biscuits	Pineapple
Wine	Mango
Sparkling Water	Dog food

How did you get on? Did the 'pointer' help you focus? As with everything else in the book, although it has been shown to work for other people, if it didn't help you, that's fine, you don't need to do it. But if it did help, you've just added another piece of kit to your study.

Now, we read...

Only when you've done all the things outlined above do you start reading the book seriously. You have a purpose for your reading now, and you know what you want to get out of each section you read.

As you read through, provided you don't mind writing in

your books, use a pencil to make little notes in the margins. If there's something you don't understand, where you'll need to do more digging, put a question mark next to it. Don't get hung up in the moment or disappear down a rabbit hole going off to do further research. Just put a mark and can come back to it later. (Sometimes reading on further will clear up the issue anyway).

If something's particularly important put a star next to it. You might find a three-star system useful. One star for, 'I want this information in my head on exam day', two stars for, 'This is really important – I'll come unstuck if I don't remember this', and three stars for, 'This could be a deal breaker if I forget it!'

Another technique which can help is to make your margin notes into questions. You'll read more about the power of questions and self-testing in chapter eight, but it's worth mentioning here. If you were reading a section about, for instance, theories of happiness. Instead of writing margin notes about the theories put forward by different researchers, you might instead put, 'What did Martin Seligman say about happiness?' When you next look at that margin note, your engage your brain in a different way by posing yourself a question like that.

Importantly, aside from little notes like these in the margins, don't make notes as you're reading. This isn't the time for notes - they come into the picture later (in the next chapter, to be precise).

There's an important reason not to make notes now - you want to get into the material and start to build up your understanding. Reading a line and stopping to make a note doesn't help that process. It all becomes much more disjointed.

Equally, don't fall into the age-old student trap of underlining or highlighting everything. Everyone loves a highlighter pen, but simply changing a page from black and white to all pink isn't going to help anyone. It might make you feel like you're making progress, but it really isn't driving you forward. If you want to highlight anything, be selective. Only pull out the most important information.

How many pages of material per mark?

I'm going to let you in on one of my own secret study tips here, and it's not necessarily one your tutors would endorse, but hey, we're friends now so why not?

Where it's possible, one of the first things I do when I'm confronted with a book for an exam is draw up a little 'pages per mark' table. I look at the syllabus and the number of marks available for each subject. Then I look at the relevant chapters of the book and work out how many pages of the book I'm going to have to read for each mark.

Sometimes, you'll find areas have an awful lot of reading, for not many marks at all. Guess where they end up in my study pecking order?

On the other hand, if there's a chapter offering lots of marks for not much reading, that gets elevated up the scale, both in priority order and in terms of how much attention I'm going to pay it.

Speed reading

Speed reading's a concept that's captured the imagination of students since it was first introduced by Evelyn Wood in the late 1950s. The average reader works between 250 and 300 words per minute, but Wood believed she could increase that between three-and-ten times over.

Since then, there have been many books and courses promising to teach you to speed read. Author Tim Ferriss believes he can help anyone to read 300% faster in just 20 minutes [1]. Meanwhile in 2007, someone read Harry Potter and the Deathly Hallows in just 47 minutes and went on to summarise it – a mere 4200 words per minute.

But does speed reading work? Well, I'll get my own experience on the table and say that it's never really worked for me. But that isn't particularly scientific, so instead, let's consider what science has to tell us.

Psychologists from various universities collaborated on a 2016 project to see whether speed reading could offer a solution They explored a range of speed reading techniques and concluded that:

"There is a trade-off between speed and accuracy in reading, as there is in all forms of behaviour. Increasing the speed with which you encounter words, therefore, has consequences for how well you understand and remember the text" [2].

They went on to say that whether speed reading works for you depends on your purpose for reading. In some cases, a drop in comprehension could be totally acceptable – for instance if you already know about the subject, but you wanted to find a particular point. Where you're not all that familiar with the material, though, and you're trying to learn it, they conclude there is no 'magic bullet'.

So, is it worth bothering or not? That's for you to decide. If you're interested in trying to learn, there are various instructional videos on YouTube and there's a good book by Tony Buzan called (oddly enough) 'The speed reading book' you might want to check out.

'Too long; didn't read' summary

- This isn't about teaching you how to read. Instead, it's about how to read with purpose. You need to get the most from the time you spend reading while you study.
- To start, consider what you're going to read. Is there a single course text you need to have, or can you select your own study material? Even where there's a set text, check whether there's an independent provider offering a more accessible version of the same thing.
- Have a goal for your reading – are you looking just to pass the exam, or do you want to become knowledgeable in the subject? They aren't the same thing, and you should approach reading differently depending on your personal goals.
- Start with the introduction and conclusion – a chapter summary, at the start or end, should give you a feel for whether this is a chapter you need to spend time on. Read those first.
- After you've read the start and finish, skim the middle – just get a feel for the content. Using a finger or pencil to guide the eye is helpful. And think about how much you already know – is this a weaker or stronger area for you?
- Once you've scanned through, read the text properly. Spend more time on areas you feel weaker, and those you expect to be worth most marks in the exam.
- Don't make notes as you read, other than little pencil notes in the margins. Try to write questions to yourself rather than just repeating the text. You

might find it useful to use question marks for things you want to come back to and stars for anything especially important.

- Speed reading is a skill some people develop. It can allow you to get more from your reading in less time, but you may find it's at the expense of your understanding.

Chapter 6

How to make meaningful notes

"*This is how you do it: sit down at the keyboard and you put one word after another until it's done. It's that easy, and that hard.*"
Neil Gaiman
"*And the idea of just wandering off to a cafe with a notebook and writing and seeing where that takes me for a while is just bliss.*"
J.K. Rowling

What's in this chapter?

IT's time to look at how to take effective notes. You'll consider the importance of structuring your notes in the right way, and how to avoid falling into common traps, like copying out the textbook. You'll also consider whether you're better off writing notes by hand or typing them.

Why make notes?

Before you look at the process of taking effective notes, you should consider why it's worth bothering with notes. (I'm always amazed at the number of people who come on training courses and make no notes at all. Some say they'll just remember the material, while others say they concentrate better if they don't make notes).

Whilst the notion of being present in the moment and listening intently to the material makes sense, the reality is that memory fades. You saw that in chapter one. You need to revisit material to 'level up' it's standing in your brain – to tell the brain it is worth hanging on to for the longer term.

Taking *relevant* notes gives you the raw material for your revision (see chapter eight). Think of it as the process of extracting meaning from your reading, or your courses. Without notes, you'll remember a portion of the material; with notes, you've got something to revisit later, to help you cement your learning for the long term. In short, a good set of notes significantly speeds up the process of revision and makes sure you're in good shape for exam day.

Copying out of a book isn't learning

So, good notes are essential. But the emphasis has to be on the word 'good', which leads to an important health warning – copying out the textbook is not learning!

Many students end up copying whole swathes of their books, effectively reproducing the entire thing on their note pad or computer. This isn't a handwriting test, nor a typing test. The only notes you need are the ones that'll be beneficial for your revision. Anything else is just a waste of time.

Your aim should be to write briefly, and in your own words, to capture sufficient information to fire up your memory banks and retrieve the important details.

The process of interacting with the material in this way

after reading starts the encoding journey – moving it from working memory toward long-term memory (chapter one).

Writing, typing, or audio?

When you're making notes, should you hand write them or type them? Well, this isn't totally straightforward – and here's why.

On the one side, many people will type their answers in the exam. Getting typing practice if you're not used to it will help you to make sure you don't lose time through terrible typing skills. However, after you've achieved a reasonable level of typing proficiency, there are several good reasons why it might be time to close your laptop and get out the old-fashioned pen and pad.

Firstly, you have to turn off the computer, which means no emails. That means fewer distractions and fewer reasons to escape study in favour of something else (emails, internet scrolling, Candy Crush).

Secondly, and perhaps more importantly, it allows you to learn better. Writing offers additional benefits through the use of more 'sensory modalities'. You interact with the words in a more direct manner. You experience the words you write in a different way.

Of course, if you're handwriting your exam that adds another dimension – it can be tough to write for a long time if you're not used to it, especially in the modern world where you probably type everything at work. Getting used to writing by hand in these circumstances is important.

So, what's the answer – type or write? Well, there's probably a place for multiple methods. You might remember in chapter four I talked about making the best use of resources, including voice-to-text software. When I'm making notes, I tend to use voice-to-text to produce my first set of notes, review these and type in any extra thoughts I want to record. These notes are then the source material for a handwritten set of notes that I use for revision using the Cornell method (see below). This combination of methods means you interact with the material in different ways and in more than one instance. And it all reinforces the learning.

If you speak the words out loud as you write them, it's even more powerful. Then you're encoding auditory cues at the same time. Major wins all round!

The time for notes

The secret here is in the order of the last two chapters – read and then note. When you're reading through, you shouldn't be writing anything other than the odd margin note or question, and highlighting should be minimal.

Once you've done that, you revisit the material and make your notes. At this point, you'll be in a better position to capture the important information from what you've read. You'll see the bigger picture and won't find yourself wasting time writing chapter-and-verse on things you don't need.

When you do make notes, the following tips might help:

1. **Make them stand out** – use colour. Coloured notes are more eye catching and more likely to invite you to read them again!
2. **Use pictures** – if you're an artistic type, draw pictures. It'll get the more artistic parts of your brain involved and double-down on your study efforts.
3. **Prioritise the key points** – if there's something important you want to remember, put

this as a first-level bullet point, then put other notes below as second order and third-order bullets.

4. **Use headings and sub-headings** – break up your notes with headings and then use sub-headings. This book uses them to make it easier to follow. Lengthy notes without sub-headings can be a bit off-putting.

5. **Paraphrase** – don't just copy someone else's words. Instead, write it in your own words. It forces your brain to process the information at a deeper level.

Note-taking in lectures and seminars

When you're in lectures or seminars, it can be hard to know what to write. You don't want to just copy down everything the tutor says (not that there's time to do that anyway).

Note-taking requires brain processing. That can be tough when you're also trying to listen and understand what's being said. Remember from chapter one that your working memory (the desktop on the computer) can only hold so much. If you're still holding what the tutor just said so you can make notes, you're not catching the new stuff they're throwing in. You get left behind, and the wheels fall off.

Despite this, research shows that taking notes in the session improves recall later. So how do you square the two?

Well, for starters, decide in advance what you're going to write. Never write out the words on the slides if you can get a copy. Perhaps just look to write down the words the tutor writes on the whiteboard or flipchart, plus anything they emphasise as being important or repeat more than once. If they do demonstrations or example calculations, those might be worth copying. Questions the tutor asks could be valuable.

It's also worth having a separate piece of paper as a 'park', where you can dump anything you don't understand in order to come back to it later, or ask the tutor about it.

Developing your own shorthand can be helpful too. Take out unnecessary words and just capture the main gist. So, for example, if the tutor says,

"The UK parliament is made up two 'houses'. The House of Commons where elected Members of Parliament (known as MPs) sit, and the House of Lords where hereditary and life peers sit. The House of Lords is known as the 'upper house' as it scrutinises the Commons",

You might reduce this to:

"Commons lower house – MPs, Lords upper house, life + hereditary."

One useful method here is (assuming you're online and can turn your mic off) quietly say the words to yourself as you write them. This increases the depth of your processing.

Cornell system

The Cornell method is a brilliant system for notetaking. It's been around for over 70 years since Walter Pauk [1] devised it at Cornell University (hence the name). It's incredibly simple can be used for lecture notes, notes on books, and notes on journal articles. It works equally well on all of them.

Quite simply, all you do is divide your page into four sections, as shown in figure 6.1, below. At the top, the title sets out either the name of the lecture the notes were taken from, the book and chapter, or the research paper.

On the right-hand side, is the box for your main notes. Here, you write bullet points taken from whichever source you're using. On the left, you have a narrower column, and here you simply write key words, taken from the content on the right. These key words should act as prompts as well as a form of index.

Finally, in the section at the bottom, you write two or three sentences summarising the notes on the page. And that's it.

```
┌─────────────────────────────────────┐
│         ┌──────────────┐            │
│         │    Title      │            │
│         └──────────────┘            │
├───────┬─────────────────────────────┤
│       │                             │
│ ┌───┐ │                             │
│ │Cue│ │   ┌──────────────────┐     │
│ │   │ │   │ Main Note Section │     │
│ │notes│ │  └──────────────────┘     │
│ └───┘ │                             │
│       │                             │
│       │   ┌──────────────────┐     │
│       │   │    Summary        │     │
│       │   └──────────────────┘     │
└───────┴─────────────────────────────┘
```

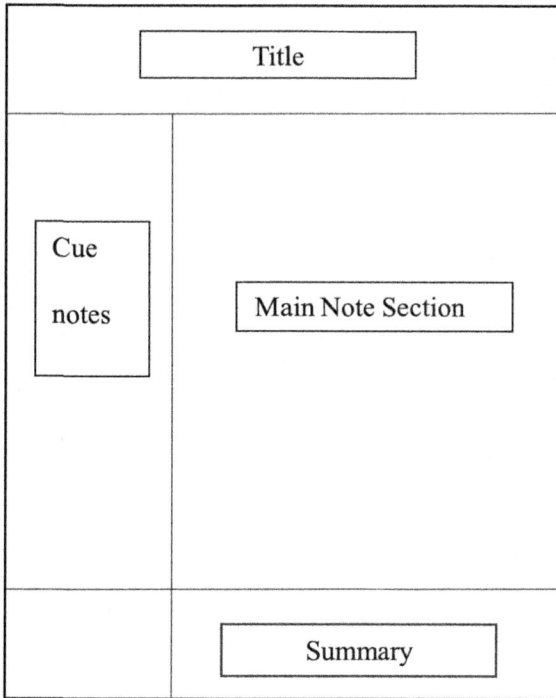

Figure 6.1 – The Cornell Note Taking Method

Let's just take a moment to emphasise the value of bullet points in the main note section. There's no point writing whole paragraphs – that just makes it harder for you to go back and review your notes in future. You want something you can read easily later and fire up your memory banks.

Equally, in the cue-notes section, you just a few words. These act as prompts for what's on the other side, while the summary box needs just enough information that, when you go back to it, you can tell whether or not this is the page you were looking for.

Below is an example of one of my own Cornell pages – my notes on an academic paper I read recently. You'll see a few things:

1. The title at the top tells you this is a paper by Ryff from 1989
2. There are 9 bullet points in the main box. They're numbered and the corresponding numbers have been added in the main paper, so you know where to find this information. This allows me to find the exact words I'm looking for.
3. Down the left, you can see key words that might be useful. Scanning these tells you this is a paper about wellbeing.
4. Finally, you can read the summary at the bottom which tells you – in my words – what this paper is all about.

It isn't neat, it isn't laid out for anyone other than me to be able to understand it – but these are my notes. They're there to help me, and I can use them to find exactly what I need when it comes to either revision (chapter eight) or writing essays (chapter seven).

Jon Dunckley

Figure 6.2 – Example of Cornell notes in action

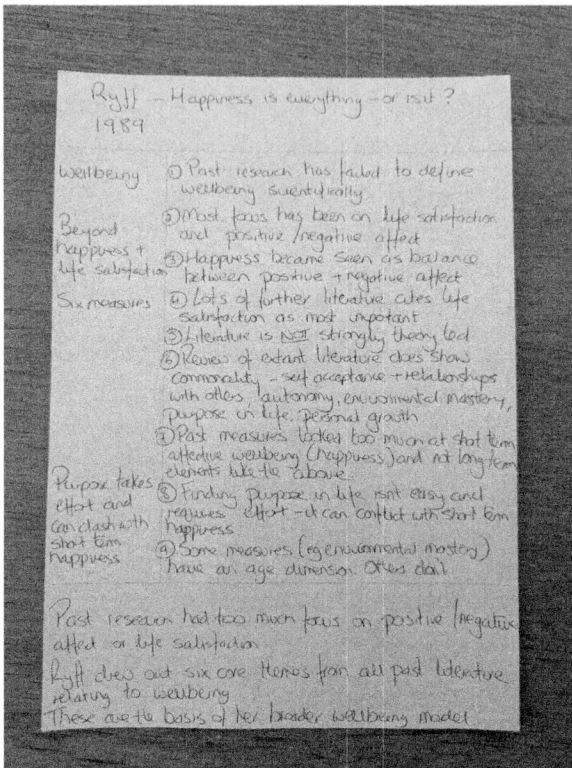

There's a mountain of research on the Cornell system, looking at students of different ages and in different types of exams. To summarise the findings, some found it improved 'smart thinking' [2], others found it helped improve confidence and reduce the impact of interruptions [3], and yet others found it more effective for retrieval than other note-taking systems in lectures [4].

Whether it will, on its own, improve exam performance is debatable [5] but there seems to be very little in the research to suggest it's going to harm your chances. Combine it with the revision techniques outlined in chapter eight and you may well find it really helpful. I certainly do.

Pictograms

As you now know, the more ways you interact with the material, the greater the chances of you remembering it. So why not have some fun? Pictograms, spider diagrams, and mind maps are all great memory aids. Creating visual aids gives you access to a different part of the brain and, as we saw in chapter one, it means you get to store the information in more than one place. The more widely the information is spread around your brain, the better the chances you'll recall it.

You don't need to make these diagrams super-complex. Whatever works for you. At the simple end, you can put a central theme in the middle of the page, then surround it with pictures that'll act as memory joggers. At the other end, you can follow the complex 'mind map method' devised and developed by Tony Buzan [6] to construct images that resemble the very neural structures you're creating the in the brain. You'll see a bit more about this in chapter eight. The important thing for now is that whatever works for you is the best method.

Understanding

The most important rule of good note taking is very simple – never write down anything you don't understand, unless you're setting yourself a task to look it up. If you haven't understood it, there's simply no point writing it down in your notes as if it makes sense. All you're doing is rolling a problem down the hill for later. When you come to revise, you still won't know what it means and you're just as likely to ignore it.

If you don't have time to look it up now, you've got two options:

1. Decide it isn't important enough to worry about and ignore it.
2. Make a note on your study plan to come back to it and pop it in your notes as a question.

In most exams, the purpose isn't to measure how much you can write down, or even how many facts you can remember – it's to see how much you understand. This is especially true when you move toward the higher-level exams (see chapter two).

Good, purposeful study is about making sure you've got the knowledge you need to be able to answer questions – even if the question isn't quite the one you were expecting. As someone wise once said – 'parrots learn, for your exam you're going to need to understand'. (OK, full disclosure, it was me who said that, but that doesn't make it any less true!)

When you really understand your subject, you're much more prone to 'brain dumping' –downloading everything you know about a subject and hoping the right answer's lurking in there somewhere. Unfortunately, as you'll see chapter ten, brain dumping seldom ends up with a good result. The examiner wants to see you answer the specific question they've set. They want your answer to be focused on the matter in hand, even if that does mean leaving out all the extra detail you have in your mind.

Once you really understand your subject, you'll find it so much easier to revise later. Facts stick much more easily when they've got meaning. The better you come to understand something, the more instinctive it becomes. Just like driving. You don't memorise each step of the driving process and recall the memory actively each time you get in the car – you just know it.

This is also important in terms of being able to 'puzzle things through' in the exam. If you get a question that you don't quite know the answer to, by really understanding your material, you're much more likely to be able to figure out some kind of answer. This is what scientists do – go back to basics or first principles and work forward using their knowledge.

So, when you finish making your notes each time make sure you ask yourself 'did I understand that?' If you didn't, you might need to come back to it again.

You can test your understanding by asking yourself questions like: what's it really about, how does it work, why does it matter, how does it fit the bigger picture? Prove to yourself you've understood it by writing a few lines before you move on.

Feynman notebook

Albert Einstein famously said, "Never believe every quote you read on the internet". OK, he didn't say that, but he did say, "If you can't explain something simply, you don't understand it well enough". And he was spot on.

One great way of following this is the 'Feynman notebook' method. This method was created by Nobel-prize winning physicist Richard Feynman, so, you know, it's got quite good breeding!

He built on the Einstein approach and developed a model to allow you to test your understanding. The model consists of just four simple steps:

1. Pick the subject where you want to test your understanding – it might be something new (for

example an area of the syllabus you're about to start studying) or something you've just finished reading about. Write the name of the topic at the top of the page.

2. Underneath the title, write down what you know about the subject, but keep it in plain English. Imagine you're trying to explain it to a 9-year old. Keep explanations simple and use examples.

3. Go back over what you've written. Look for any areas that feel weak or woolly. Look for areas that don't completely make sense. Those are likely to be the ones you haven't 100% understood.

4. Go over it again and simplify your work from step 2. Make the language simpler, see if you can use analogies and relate the material to other concepts.

If you can do this and all you're left with is something you'd feel comfortable explaining to the next-door neighbour's child, or my mum, you've probably got it!

Not many researchers have put this method to the test – perhaps the provenance of it puts them off. Those who have tested it found it to be effective [7], and it does seem to work well.

Review

Whatever method you use, when you've finished making notes, go back over them straight away, before ending your study session. This is a good time to play your 'trigger song' again (chapter one) to help the memories bed in.

Ask yourself whether you've hit your objectives for the session. Was there anything you didn't get around to? Anything you didn't understand and noted down to look into later? If so, that's fine, just make sure those things go on your study planner, so they don't fall through the cracks.

Then, once you've finished, congratulate yourself on a job well done!

Jon Dunckley

'Too long; didn't read' summary

- Note-taking is an important study skill. However good you think your memory is, without taking notes, you'll find revision an awful lot harder.
- Copying the entire book isn't the answer – you need to be selective with the notes you make. Only write the important stuff.
- Hand-written, typed, and voice-to-text notes all have a place. Mix it up according to the needs of your exam, but handwritten notes are especially powerful for memory.
- Use colour, pictures and headings to break things up. Try to write in bullets rather than lengthy paragraphs, and paraphrase things in your own words – it'll mean more when you go back to them.
- The Cornell Method is a powerful way to take notes. It involves dividing your paper into sections: a header, a main notes box, key words from the notes, and a summary.
- Don't write down things you don't understand – it's a waste of time. The Feynman notebook system is helpful for checking how well you understand something and how simply you can explain it.

Chapter 7

Coursework and essays

"The two most powerful warriors are patience and time" Leo Tolstoy

""I love deadlines. I love the whooshing noise they make as they go by." Douglas Adams

What's in this chapter?

IN THIS CHAPTER, you'll look at assessment by coursework and essay, which require different skills from examinations. You'll see how important it is to plan your approach, the benefit of stepping away when your mind gets stuck, and the dangers of plagiarism (also known as cheating!)

A different skill

This book is predominantly about studying for traditional exams. Yet, in the modern world many assessments will have at least some element of coursework, so it would be remiss not to include a brief chapter on the skills involved in writing essays and other coursework submissions.

The process of writing an essay outside the exam hall is necessarily more involved than one you write in the heat of an exam setting. With more time to prepare, your examiners expect more depth and more consideration of your answer. (I'll be honest, I'm a strange one – I really enjoy exams, and I enjoy writing essays just as much, but the skills involved aren't quite the same).

The good news is that much of what you've covered so far – the skills of reading with purpose and taking good notes – help just as much with your coursework submissions as with your exam preparation, so you're already a good distance down the line to getting them done!

Don't let time get away

The most important guidance when it comes to essays and course work is that you should not, repeat you _should not_, leave it until the last minute. But then you wouldn't do that, now would you? Thought not.

So often, students meander their way through the weeks, paying little attention to the essay they're supposed to be writing. Then, as the final deadline approaches, they launch into a full-scale panic. They snatch at the work and, invariably, turn in half-baked essays well below the standard of their capabilities. Not ideal.

Just as you read about the importance of planning for exams in chapter three, so the same applies for coursework and essay deadlines. Start from the end date and work backwards. Make sure you build in time for research, drafting your submission and editing. It can also be a good idea to build in a day or two between drafting and editing, just to 'live with' your work for a while – you'll see why, shortly.

One technique I particularly like here comes from some people very close to my heart. As a couple, they're very similar on most things, but they differ significantly when it comes to punctuality. He never likes to be late for anything, whereas if she knows she needs to be somewhere at 6.30, she's liable to start getting ready at 6.29. What's their solution? Whatever time they need to be there, he tells her they need to be there half an hour earlier. You can follow this same approach for your work by telling yourself your deadline is a week earlier than it really is. Work back from the earlier date and you've got built-in wiggle room.

What does good look like?

If you want to get the best marks, you need to know what's expected of you and then deliver it.

There was a lot about understanding the syllabus in chapter two and, when it comes to essays and coursework, this may be even more important.

Generally, examiners set a 'marking rubric.' This breaks down the requirements for the work into different sections and then specifies what's expected of the student at each level. An excerpt of an example rubric is shown below (figure 7.1).

Criterion	Distinction	Merit	Pass	Fail
Content (40%)	Exceptionally well researched, shows great insight and deep understanding	Well research with well-reasoned argument, backed by adequate research	Lacks sufficient research and presents weak or inconsistent argument	Lacks research and argument is either poor or absent
Organisation (30%)	Clear and unambiguous flow, excellent structure leading the reader	Well organised with clear sections and linkage between sections	Lacks organisation, sections not clearly separated, limited links between sections	Lack of organisation, no coherent narrative
Style and clarity (15%)	Exceptionally clear and engaging, encourages reading, free of grammatical or stylistic error	Mostly very well written with few grammatical or stylistic errors	Numerous stylistic or grammatical errors distracting from the flow	Filled with stylistic and grammatical errors such that it is difficult to follow
Referencing (15%)	Excellent range of external references. Layout of referencing fully compliant	Strong range of external referencing, layout mostly or fully compliant	Limited range of external referencing, layout mostly non-compliant	Insufficient range of external references, layout mostly or fully non-compliant

Figure 7.1 – Example Marking Rubric

From this, it's clear that, whilst content and organisation are worth the lion's share of the marks, a significant proportion (30%) is tied to clarity and accuracy, and the quality of referencing. Simply getting your referencing right and carefully proofreading your submission would potentially earn you 30% of the overall marks.

This is a very simplistic rubric, admittedly, but even the more complex ones give a clear indication of what's expected of students. Following this from the outset is important if you want to gain the highest marks.

When it comes to essays, the rubric should be your first port of call. For an essay I wrote recently, it was divided into 'knowledge and understanding', 'analysis and criticality', 'application and practice', and 'transferable skills'. It also identified that areas like accurate referencing, explaining jargon and staying within the required wordcount were being given the same standing as the strength of my argument.

Tell a story

A good essay or report should tell a story. The reader should be able to clearly see the argument you're making, the research that lies behind it, and the conclusions you've drawn.

If you want to make sure you're giving them that story, you've got to start with your storyboard. Less prepared students dive in and start writing before they've planned out the structure and, as a result, their output is disjointed and doesn't flow.

Let me fill you in on a secret. When I decided to write this book, the first thing I did was plan out the topics I wanted to cover. I broke these into sections, and then chapters. Each chapter had some headings – things I knew I wanted to talk about – and then I wrote bullet point notes for the content under each heading.

The outline of the book was there before a single complete paragraph had been written. It made it easy to see how to connect sections and chapters, and where content would be relevant to more than one area. It also allowed me to change the structure and move chapters around until the flow worked. It's the same for essays – first of all, drop in your headings, then sub-headings, then outline content, and only then do you start writing.

If you find this difficult, structuring your essay is one area in which AI can be really useful. In chapter four, you saw the warning about being careful and not cheating with it. But programmes like ChatGPT or Bard are often able to suggest a logical and coherent narrative for an essay. Then, you just need to slot in your own words.

Write, then prune

Most essays have a set word count. Don't get too hung up on this to begin with. The best strategy, once you've got your outline structure, is to start writing. Write the entire essay according to the headings you've put in place, paying no attention to the wordcount.

Invariably, you'll end up with too many words. That's when you start to prune.

Go back and look at what you've written. Ask yourself whether there are any unnecessary sentences. Is there anything you can chop out? Where can words be removed? Sometimes just contracting words can save you as much as 5% of a word count (is not becomes isn't – that one word saved!)

Referencing and plagiarism

Most students know what plagiarism is, but in case you're unfamiliar, plagiarism is defined by the University of Oxford as, "Presenting work or ideas from another source as your own, with or without consent of the original author, by incorporating it into your work without full acknowledgement" [1]. Let's be quite clear – it's a bad thing! Copying someone else's work in this way (or, in some exams, even your own past work) is cheating and there are sophisticated software packages designed to catch students in the act.

Many institutions use software called 'Turnitin'. Students submit their work through this package, which then searches the work against its databases, scoring the student's submission for the degree of duplication it finds. The database it uses is vast, including the internet, academic journals, and student papers.

If the software finds a high degree of duplication, it'll flag the work for the institution to look at in more detail, and that often spells trouble for the student.

To avoid being accused of cheating, it's vital you reference any work you've taken from elsewhere. For example, the quote above refers to Oxford University as the source for the definition of plagiarism. At the back of the book, you'll find the full details of where this definition was taken from. I've given the University of Oxford full credit for the statement I've borrowed and haven't tried to pass it off as my own.

Each assessing body has its preferred method for writing up references, and you might hear of the 'Harvard System', the 'Chicago System', or the 'American Psychological Association' system. It's important you find out which referencing system is used by your examining body, and then make sure you reference in the correct format. It isn't at all unusual for 10 or even 15% of the overall mark to be awarded just for the quality of your referencing!

Jon Dunckley

Unstick yourself

Sometimes, despite all your best efforts, you just can't seem to make any progress. You get the outline for a piece of work, and you know broadly what you want to say, but you just can't get going. You've probably heard of 'writer's block'. It's something that impacts all kinds of people, including some very famous authors, so you shouldn't feel bad if you experience a touch of it when you're trying to get that assignment together.

The solution to overcoming writer's block is actually quite simple. You need to step away from it. In fact, moving away from your work like this can have powerful psychological effects on more than one level.

Firstly, there's something called the Ovsiankina effect [2] which says humans have a strong urge to finish things once we get started (that explains why I keep watching some of those awful box sets on Netflix!). By stopping partway through the task, your motivation to come back to it increases. Often, when you're suffering from a block, that extra motivation can be a real boost.

Secondly, stepping away allows your mind to work on the issue in the background (something Graham Wallas calls 'incubation' [3]). In this, now classic, work, he argued creativity has four stages. You 'prepare', then you 'incubate' (ponder on the matter). This leads to 'illumination' (your lightbulb moment) and finally to 'verification' (making sure you've not got the wrong end of the stick).

This process can be really powerful when putting together your assignments. Get your outline together, but when you get stuck, move away from it. Do something else – watch some TV, go for a walk with the dog, play some sport. (Personally, I'll often go to the gym, have a swim, sit in the steam room for a while, and grab a coffee. In fact, much of this book has been put

116

together in that very setting!) More often than not, when you come back, you can pick up the work with new insights and carry on much more easily than before you went.

So, if you find yourself struggling, don't worry; just down tools and do something else. Your brain will look after you and it'll keep working on your behalf. You just concentrate on relaxing, and when you come back amazing things can happen!

'Too long; didn't read' summary

- Coursework and essays require a slightly different skillset from exams, but the groundwork's very similar.
- Make sure you start in plenty of time and have a clear timeline for completion – aim to be done early to give yourself some wiggle room.
- Know what good looks like – the marking 'rubric' is a source of very useful information.
- Structure before you write – if you're struggling, AI can help, but be careful not to ask it to write everything for you.
- Write freely, then prune. It's easier to cut down to the word count than to try to hit it as you go.
- If you're using other people's work, make sure you give them credit – referencing is the difference between good research, and cheating.
- When you get stuck, step away. The process of 'incubation' means the brain often finds creative solutions while you're busy doing other things.

3. The big day approaches

Chapter 8

How to revise

"The best way out is always through" Robert Frost
"I dunno..." Scooby Doo

What's in this chapter?

As the exam draws closer, good revision is essential. This chapter covers how to revise, and the most common mistakes students make when revising. You'll read about a range of revision techniques backed by scientific research. These are proven to be effective at getting information to stick. Different techniques will suit different people, so you won't need to use them all – just find the ones that work for you.

A pile of papers

Whatever techniques you've been using, you'll likely reach a point where you've built up a whole wad of notes. Hopefully, they'll be good notes and you'll have used the Cornell method (chapter six) but even so, lots of notes don't translate into a lot of exam success without something in between. That's where good revision technique comes in.

Your very first goal should be to get your ducks in a row. Sort out those notes. Categorise them into topics, and number your pages. Make sure all the content in the notes is accurate – you don't want to be learning things that aren't right. Invest a bit of time in your organisation – it makes what follows a lot easier.

You've also got to be honest with yourself about where the notes have taken you. How comfortable do you currently feel?

Some areas will have properly sunk in. You'll feel comfortable with your knowledge. Others will need more work to get them to stick in your mind – especially where you've taken lots of notes from courses or from watching videos.

This chapter is all about that middle part – the crucial actions that lie between initial study and exam.

Where are you?

Before you begin, grade yourself on your current level of knowledge. You can do this by working through the syllabus and asking yourself whether you'd rate each area as an 'A', 'B', or 'C', just as you did before you started reading (chapter five). This time, though, you need to be a bit harder on yourself:

- A – Grade yourself as an 'A' if you feel you could go into an exam tomorrow and answer questions on this subject. You think this is a real strong suit for you, and you're ready to go.
- B – When you rate yourself as a 'B' you feel reasonably comfortable, but know you still need to do more brushing up.

- C – And 'C' indicates you really don't feel comfortable. You know you need to put in more effort on this subject.

This gives you a really good indication of where you need to invest time during your revision.

You can cross reference this against where you expect the most marks to be available. If you've rated an area as 'C' but the syllabus tells you there will only be 3 out of 100 questions on this subject, you might decide to review this a bit further down the pecking order. Equally, if a 'B' subject is worth 10 out of the 100 questions, it's worth investing extra time there.

If you look at an area and don't even feel you could give yourself a 'C', in other words you just don't get it, you've got two options:

1. Let it go. If it's something you can afford to let slide, don't get hung up on it, just let it go and devote your time to other areas.
2. Get help. Talk to your tutor, other students, or go to the web and see if anyone has explained it there in a way that makes more sense.

One note of caution here. Just because you've graded yourself as an 'A' on an area, don't ignore it in your studies. You'll still need to revise it; you might just allocate less time to that revision.

Many students fall victim to what psychologists call the 'fluency illusion' when it comes to exam day. Areas they thought they knew turn out to be less familiar than they'd expected. By including your stronger areas in your study, you can help avoid this.

One nice exercise to help with this is the KWLQ model [1].

- What do you **K**now?
- What do you **W**ant to know?
- What have you **L**earned?
- What **Q**uestions remain?

You saw in chapter one that linking information to things you already know is powerful for memory, so make sure you've got the 'big rocks' in first. Then you can in-fill with the extra details.

Break it up

You need to plan your revision, just like you planned your initial study. Give yourself time and, when you're planning, it can also help to write the location where you intend to complete that study session. Having a location gives extra accountability and makes it more likely you'll get it done.

By the way, did you know that you're more likely to win the Eurovision song contest if you go first or last?

"No, Jon. I didn't. But can we get back to revision, please..."

I'm not losing it, it's all related. Your brain remembers the first and last things you encounter more than what goes in the middle. Why do you think I've bookended the chapters with what you're going to cover and what you just covered? You can make good use of this. For each study session, plan to tackle the most difficult material at the start and the end of the session. You'll stand significantly more chance of remembering it that way.

Research also tells us that you learn at least as much, but you *remember* more, when you space out your learning, rather than when you try to do it all in large chunks. So, you should separate out your revision into chunks - topics and sub-topics and build this into your plan. Map out the big picture, get the framework, then hang things on it.

Scientists have known this to be true for many years, but it hasn't made its way into mainstream education. There's one important reason for this - it is too hard to get students to do the work once, let alone do it multiple times! Thankfully, you're in control of your own destiny, so you're able to maximise your chances by employing the most effective strategies.

In chapter one, you learned how the memory works, including the power of reinforcement. You might remember 'Jost's law' which says reinforcing something straight away after you study it isn't the most effective way to help it stick. Instead, you need to review it periodically, at spaced intervals.

The optimum reinforcement schedule is to look at your work after one day, one week, and one month [2]. Nobody really knows why this works so well, but researchers seem to broadly agree that it does. It could be that reviewing things in this way strengthens the signal to the brain that this is something of importance, and therefore worth keeping. The initial reinforcement tells the brain to hang on to it for a while. At the one-week point, the brain's starting to wonder whether it can let it go, but the extra reinforcement tells it the information's still worth keeping, so it boosts its importance and reschedules forgetting for a month down the line. When you then come back to it a month later, the brain finally gets the idea – this is something that needs to be retained indefinitely.

Inevitably, as the gaps between reviews get longer, you'll find you've forgotten more information each time, and need to reinforce more. This in itself is useful because it provides you with a 'to learn' list for your ongoing revision.

As if this weren't enough, there's also another benefit. Each time you review the material, you'll be adding new 'contextual cues' and linking more information from your surroundings to the learning, allowing it to be recalled more easily (see chapter one). This means you'll be tagging that information to more neural networks in the brain, increasing the chances of you hanging on to it.

Take a break

Having breaks in your study can be beneficial on a number of levels. In the last chapter I talked about the Ovsiankina effect (the natural urge to finish things once you've started). Here, I'll raise you the 'Zeigarnik effect' [3]. This says if you interrupt something, you make it more memorable. So, stopping halfway through a topic of revision and taking a break is likely to make that material more memorable and increase the chances of you remembering it later. And the beauty? You'll come back from your break, because the Ovsiankina effect won't let you leave it!

A secondary benefit from breaks in study is they allow you to exercise and, as you saw in chapter one, exercise promotes blood flow to the brain and increases dopamine production, which fuels memory. So, step away periodically and go for a walk. It helps.

Review before sleep

Whatever time of day you revise, try to incorporate a little look through your material before bed. Remember, the hippocampus really comes out to play when you're sleeping, and it works overtime to reinforce your learning. Give it the tools it needs and let it do its thing.

Relate to the test

When you're deciding on your revision approach, be sure to ask yourself how you need to use this information. Remember Bloom's taxonomy from chapter two? If you're required to 'know' something, you need to study it to a lower level than if you're being asked to 'analyse' it, and that means a different amount of work.

Understanding is everything

The goal of study is to get yourselves to the point where you can explain things simply to your examiner by answering their questions. The better you understand it, the better your chances in the exam – it's that simple. So, everything you do in revision should be about both remembering AND understanding. Just committing things to memory without true understanding isn't going to get the results.

In chapter six, you looked at note taking. One of the important lessons then was never write down anything you don't understand. This is where that becomes vital. If you've got pages of notes that all make perfect sense, you've got a basis from which to start your revision.

If, however, you've ignored the sage advice of chapter six and spent hours studiously copying out text from your book without understanding what you're writing, well you're going to have a harder time with the revision stage of passing your exam. And you're far more likely to be derailed if the questions don't fall exactly as you're hoping.

Let's go back to the notebook system, (chapter six) developed by Nobel-prize winning scientist Richard Feynman. He built on Einstein's view that if you can't explain something simply, you don't understand it well enough.

Real understanding comes from being able to explain it to someone who knows nothing about the subject, because you're required to manipulate the information in your brain at a much more complex level than simply repeating it.

If you can explain it to your nanna, or your young nephew, you're in good shape! That might be a stretch, but if you've got a supportive partner, try teaching them (unless they already know it, in which case have them test you).

When you do this, try to cover these elements:

- What is it?
- What does it mean?
- Why does it matter?
- How does it relate to something else?

If you can cover all these, you should be confident in your knowledge.

Most common revision mistakes

This is not an exhaustive list, but these are the most common mistakes made by students when revising:

1. *Not doing it!*

I know, I know, you'd never fall into this group, but you'd be surprised how many students do. They simply never get around to doing the revision. Either they set themselves an unrealistic schedule, or they fail to adapt their schedule to meet the needs of the real world.

Remember, you must fix on the goal – passing the exam – but be flexible on the route to get there.

If you don't put in the time, you won't get the results.

Remember the path through the snow from chapter one? To make those memories stick, you need to keep on walking up and down that path. Eventually, you'll clear enough snow for the path to be fully established. If you stop, new snowfall will soon cover up your footprints.

2. Treating study as two entirely separate phases

Many students treat study as two distinct phases. In the first phase you gather information. In the second, you try to get that information into your heads. If you blend the two, by beginning the reinforcement process earlier in the journey, you'll find you need to do less revision at the end.

Set aside time for those one-day and one-week initial reviews and by the time you get to the one-month point and you're in the revision mode, you'll find it a lot easier.

3. Trying to learn everything – remember not all knowledge is created equal

One of my favourite sayings is, "Don't let perfect be the enemy of good'. You don't need to cover absolutely everything. Many students leave themselves insufficient time for revision because they're busy trying to devour each page of the textbook down to the minutiae. Not all subjects are of equal importance. Concentrate on the big rocks, the subjects you definitely need and fill in the gaps later.

*4. Thinking that just re-reading your notes will be enough –
especially if you don't understand it*

This is probably the worst mistake of all. Students sat with
hundreds of pages of notes, just reading them over and over
again, hoping the information will somehow stick. It isn't likely
to work, and if you've written stuff down without properly
understanding it, it's even less likely to.

Remember chapter one, and how the brain works. Just
reading those notes requires very little processing power. Not
many neural networks are fired up, and the connections made
between the different parts of your brain will start to fade.
Instead, you need to learn it in a 'brain friendly' and engaging
manner – that'll have the neural networks lighting up like
Christmas.

Revision techniques that work

If just re-reading your notes isn't the way forward, what is?
Well, there are many techniques that students have found
effective over the years. Here are 12 to choose from. Have a
play with them, see which ones fit your own mind best and try
to use a few. Mix it up. Challenge your brain to learn in
different ways and it'll reward you. The aim is to process the
information in as many different ways as possible.

Try speaking out loud as you do revise – you'll engage more
than one part of the brain. Get hands-on, write on paper, draw
pictures, use colour – red for one topic, blue for another – the
more bits of your brain you get involved, the better your
chances of recall.

I might not buy into the idea of 'learning styles' (chapter
one) but I certainly buy into the idea you enjoy certain activities more, and you tend to get more out of things you enjoy.

. . .

1. Testing – the daddy of all techniques

I'm giving you this one first because in my opinion, and the opinion of many researchers, it's the biggie. If there's one technique that I'd put money on making a difference to your success, it is testing.

Earlier in this chapter, you read about the fluency illusion – the belief you know things because you've looked at them often. If you want to protect yourself from this phenomenon, testing is the key. Putting yourself on the spot shows how strong you are and which areas you still need to brush up on.

Importantly, testing can be done throughout the learning process. There's evidence that giving yourself a mock test before you start studying helps your brain to sift and store information better when you do start to study (chapter two). It makes you engage with material in a different way, especially if you follow up with the learning quickly after.

So, how can you make best use of this? Well, here are some ideas:

- Start each session with a mini test based on what you covered last time and what you're about to cover. Both will help.
- End each study session with a mini test based on what you've just covered.
- Form study groups with other students and test each other
- Ask your tutor to set you extra questions
- Look for packs of questions that are available from third-party suppliers

And then there's the biggie – use past papers from the examiner. Past paper practice is often what helps students pass their exams. But there's a caveat – past papers work best when you follow up and find out the 'why' for questions you get wrong. Use them as learning opportunities.

One thing to consider – giving your notes to someone else and asking them to develop questions helps promote their neural pathways, not yours. The person asking needs to read, process, weigh-up, and develop questions, using many centres in the brain. Most of your activity is passive. You hear the question which results in some processing, but with repeated testing you just end up recognising the question and generating the answer from the same area of the brain, so there's not much distributed processing involved. It's more powerful for them to ask you questions which require you to present something back to them or explain it as if they were a toddler (Feynman notebook style).

2. The blank sheet

This is so simple.

All you need to do is take a blank sheet of paper and at the top write the name of a topic (much as you did for the Feynman notebook system). Then, under that topic, just write down as much as you can remember. Get it all out on the page. Bullet points work best so you're not writing war and peace but keep going until you're done.

Once you feel you've written down everything you know, ask your brain to find a little extra and look for one or two more things to write. Then, and this is the clever bit, put it to one side and do the same exercise for a few more subjects, before going back to the first and seeing if you've found more information.

Think about it – this is the process you'll follow in exams. You'll need to access certain information about a subject, and you won't know which bits until you get in there, so you want to have it all available. In the exam you'll often come back to questions when your brain's had extra thinking-time (see chapters ten and eleven).

This exercise sets your brain up for the type of mental activity exam day's going to call for, and it shows you the areas where you're strong and weak. There's nothing that says, 'best read up on this' like having a piece of paper with only three bullet points on it!

3. Summaries and Cornell

Summarising is another powerful technique that works for many students. In fact, this was the main technique I used when I first started studying at school. I'd take my notes and reduce them down to a shorter summary. Then I'd take that summary and try to summarise it further. I'd repeat this process until I was down to a dozen or so words on the page. OK, full disclosure, my original intention was to make myself a cheat sheet, so small I could slip it under my watch and smuggle it in. I never claimed to be an angel. Of course, I never needed to cheat because by the time I'd summarised and then summarised those summaries, I'd learned the content. I could go into the exam cheat-sheet free and with a clear conscience.

You can employ the summarising technique in a slightly more sophisticated manner with the Cornell note taking system from chapter six. With the summary box on the bottom, and the cue notes down the left-hand side, review your learning by looking in the first instance at the cue notes and seeing how much you remember. If you don't remember enough, go to the summary. If that doesn't work, go to the main notes. If you're still struggling, go back to the source information.

Repeating this approach helps the information link to those cue words so eventually just thinking of the cues opens up the broader information for you.

You could also try using verbal versions of Cornell with a voice recorder. Have a keyword, then pause, then play the next bit.

4. Pictures

Pictures are an interesting one. As you know from chapter one, we have different types of memory, and visual memory is stored in a different part of the brain. Making good use of pictures in your study can help you to maximise the benefit of that extra part of the brain which won't otherwise be used.

Now, in the interests of full disclosure, I should tell you this doesn't work for me. I'm one of the (approximately) 4% of people who is 'aphantasic', which means I don't have the ability to generate mental images. For me, using pictures to study would be largely a waste of time as I can't generate the image again later. But that's the point of having all these different techniques – different things work for different people.

One of my old clients was a painter. He used to paint land-scapes and when he couldn't sleep at night, he'd lie in bed vividly picturing himself flying around one of the pyramids in Egypt, watching the way the light bounced off different surfaces. For him, visualisation was a powerful tool for memory, and he made great use of a particular technique called 'Mind Maps'.

In chapter six, we talked about Mind Maps - the creation of Tony Buzan, one of the world's leading experts on memory. These are now in common use and have been adapted in many ways. The basic principle is quite simple. You make your notes in a form that resembles the way the brain's connected. You have a central concept in the middle, then you branch out from this in the same way a neural connection builds up in the brain.

You start with the core topic, then work out the subtopics

relating to this core, and how the different subtopics link to each other. Then you plot them out on the page, using those connections, and include both words and pictures to increase your storage potential of the information.

What you end up with is a set of study notes physically resembling the wiring of your brain. If you're interested in looking in more detail at these, have a quick look at the Wikipedia page for mind maps – it has examples in different formats. You might want to give a few a try. Alternatively, you could look out Tony Buzan's book on the subject, appropriately entitled 'Mind Map Mastery'.

5. Go Sherlock

Sherlock Holmes, probably the most famous fictional detective of all time, was noted for his incredible memory. And it was based on a very special approach to storing information that many people could use – the memory palace.

The idea, in simple terms, is to imagine a house – it could be your home, or if you're like Sherlock and you've got the capacity for a palace, knock yourself out. Each room in that house is used to store information. So, in the kitchen, you might mentally pin notes to the kettle, the toaster, the microwave, the coffee machine. In the fridge you might store more information. All around that room, you imagine key pieces of information you want to remember being stored.

Imagine your job is to remember the last 10 monarchs of the UK and the dates of their reign. You might decide this is a job for the living room. King Charles III might be the dog (a King Charles Cavalier) with a big '2022 – to now' around his neck. On the armchair in the corner is Queen Elizabeth II, wearing a cardboard sign saying 1952-2022, while on the TV is EastEnders and under the Queen Victoria sign is '1837 to 1901'.

The more vivid you make these pictures and the content of the room, the easier it is to recall the information.

Since each room is used to store particular information, you only access the things you need when you walk into a that specific mental room of your memory palace.

If you think about it, this is very similar to the technique of studying in different places – you're linking information to various location cues in the brain. Essentially, you're doing the same thing, but in virtual reality.

6. Or maybe Line of Duty...

To stay with detectives for a while, you might decide to come out of Sherlock's era and move toward a more 'line of duty' approach, using a crime board. In the TV show they have all the relevant clues pinned to a white board and lines creating associations between different things.

You can do this at home if you've got space. Create a memory wall for the exam. Put key words from your Cornell notes on pieces of paper or card, draw pictures, print out relevant quotes, whatever you'll need. Importantly, the things on your wall should be prompts only – you want your brain to do the work. Don't put detailed notes up there or you won't benefit from the exercise.

Each time you visit the wall, take something down, spend time looking at it and asking yourself what you can remember about it. If you find you don't remember enough, put that on your schedule for revision in the next few days, and then revisit it.

Over time, as you remember more and more, change what lives on the wall. Retire the things that you're comfortable with and add in areas you want to work on. Make the wall a living, breathing thing.

7. The brain loves stupid

When I do one-to-one tutoring, I always take my Cookie Monster soft toy. I sit him in his own chair and ask my student to stand in front of him and present to him the things they are struggling to remember.

Why? Well, apart from the fact that it's great fun to watch, it's also an amazing memory aid. The brain is wired to remember the unusual. It makes sense when you think about it – unusual things were potentially threats to our ancestors. Our brains are tuned to look out for them.

Because the experience of presenting to Cookie Monster is so bizarre, it sticks in the mind. When the student gets to the exam, they imagine themselves back in front of Cookie and they'll almost always remember the things they told him.

You can use this yourself. Try explaining things to your cat, interviewing yourself about them in the shower, or chatting them through with your toddler's Gruffalo. The more 'out there' the scenario, the greater the stickiness of the memory, so play around with this one and find your own version of daft.

8. Old school revision cards

There's a reason some techniques have persisted for decades, and, in this case, it's because they work – but only if you use them right.

Some students wander around with wads of revision cards crammed full of notes. That's not revision cards – that's small bits of note paper! You can do better than that.

To make the best use of revision cards, think more like Trivial Pursuit ®. The classic board game uses question cards which have the questions on one side and the answer on the other. That's the perfect approach.

On the one side put some notes – not too much (think along the lines of the summary and key words from the Cornell note-taking system). You just want enough information, so it acts as a memory jogger.

Then, on the other side of the card, write yourself questions that relate to those notes. When you come to use the card, read the questions, see if you can answer them, and then check your answers using the notes on the other side.

Remember, testing is the absolute king of revision methods. This way, you're using testing in conjunction with your study prompts, and you can carry those cards around with you, to test yourself at will.

If you want to be a bit less 'old school' and a bit more 'new school', you can also make electronic flashcards online. Just do a quick Google search to find them.

9. Back to music

Think of a song. Any song. Start to play it in your head. I'm doing it right now, Wonderwall by Oasis. Feel free to join in, "I said maybe..."

You can all do it.

Now think of a poem.

Not so easy. At a push I might be able to give you a few lines of the Invictus poem. (If you don't know it, do look it up, it's a fantastically moving piece of poetry – Idris Elba did a great version of it for the Invictus games, but I digress...)

What about a passage of text from a book you've read in the past. Just four or five lines. What? Can't do that one? Nor me.

You might read thousands of books, but very few of us could repeat more than a few lines from any of them word-for-word. Even classics, books you've read multiple times. You can often share the gist but not the actual words.

So why is it that you can sing at least a verse and a chorus of Aqua's Barbie Girl, but only muster a few lines of your favourite poem and not more than one or two lines of Pride and Prejudice?

In short – music.

The brain finds it much easier to remember things linked to music. Back in chapter one, you read about trigger songs – linking your study to a particular song to help recall. You can take that further by linking specific pieces of information to specific songs. If you're struggling to remember a list of things, change the lyrics of a song you know well, to incorporate those words.

Let me give you an example.

Years ago, I saw stage illusionist Derren Brown live. Part of the act involved him predicting items and then the order in which they'd appear. It was a long and complex (although very impressive) routine but what sticks in my mind is the end. To the tune of their hit 'Obviously', the band McFly appeared on the screen singing, "Obviously, the order will be, an egg and a needle, and then an ice-cream. And there'll be moose, and goose, and apple juice, oh yeah!"

It's been a long time since that show and I only heard it once, but I still remember it (despite my best endeavours to forget it) Give it a try, you'll be surprised how easily you can set information to music even if, like me, you can't play a note!

10. Mnemonics

Mnemonic (nem-on-ick) is the rather grand name given to any form of learning technique that helps you remember something. They're usually words, pictures, systems, or tools that help with storage and retrieval of facts, phrases, or names.

Many students make wide use of mnemonics in their study and most people use them in their daily lives without thinking about it. How do you remember the colours of the rainbow? Many people use ROY GB IV (an acronym) or Richard Of

York Gave Battle In Vain (an acrostic) to help them remember Red, Orange, Yellow, Green, Blue, Indigo, Violet.

How about the planets in the solar system? My Very Easy Method Just Speeds Up Nothing (Mars, Venus, Earth, Jupiter, Saturn, Uranus, Neptune).

I used one writing this book. When I was writing chapter one – memory – I was struggling to get the right structure. I took some time out and went to the gym for a swim. While I was there, I realised the structure I wanted to follow was to cover short-and-long term memory, then move on to looking at the role of the hippocampus and neuroplasticity. But I was worried I'd forget before I got home. What did I do? I just committed to memory a camera and a plasticine hippo! The camera was for SLR (a type of camera but also short and long run memory), the plasticine hippo was neuroplasticity and the hippocampus. When I decided I wanted to follow up with information on reinforcement, that was a group of soldiers busting into the gym. Sure enough, when I got home, it was still there (and it was still there two weeks later).

That's the beauty of mnemonics. They can be words, images, concepts, symbols, whatever works for you. They can be full of colour, light, even sound.

You might find they work especially well when you're trying to remember lists. You take the first letter of each item on the list and try to form them into a word. So, for instance, if you were trying to remember the following shopping list:

- Milk
- Pasta
- Bananas
- Cheese
- Tea

Jon Dunckley

- Oil
- Avocado
- Onions

you might turn them into 'MOP BOAT C'

It can be strangely satisfying to put them into anagrams or other mnemonics.

This is another area where AI can be really helpful. Pop the things you want to form into a mnemonic into ChatGPT or Bard and ask for help. They often produce some crackers. For example, based on the above shopping list, ChatGPT offered: Bob's Cat Took A Mooch Outside On The Porch!

11. Interleaved practice

The concept of interleaved practice has become more popular in schools and colleges over recent years. Put simply, it's about mixing up subjects so that instead of spending a whole study session looking at one topic, you spend part of it on topic A and part on topic B.

The science is quite simple. Forcing your brain to switch between subjects makes it work harder and more closely replicates the skills required in your exam.

The science behind it originated in getting kids to throw beanbags [2]. One group of children practiced throwing bean bags at a target three feet away. Another group spent half their time practicing on a target two feet away and half on a target four feet away. After several weeks of practice, all were tested on their ability to hit the three feet target. Despite having spent none of their time on that target before, the mixed group performed better. The challenge of mixing between two-and-four feet targets had forced them to learn the skill at a deeper level.

While the beanbag study connects to motor movement, similar studies found more cerebral tasks followed a similar pattern. Mixing up activities promotes better learning across the board.

One of the key benefits of such mixing-and-matching appears to be that you don't become overconfident. It comes back to the fluency illusion. When you just do one thing, you can become overconfident in your ability. By mixing it up, you have a slower perceived rate of learning, but actually learn quicker overall. This, in itself, is worth noting as a point of caution – students often believe 'block learning' (working on a single subject) is more effective, simply because it *feels* better. The science, however, suggests it's less effective overall than mixing it up.

12. Elaborative interrogation

Ever tried to have a conversation with a three-year-old? If you have, you'll know they have favourite words: 'Why?' and 'What?' They ask them all the time. And why (see what I did there?) do they do that? Well, because it's a cracking way to learn.

The slightly pompous sounding, technique of 'elaborative interrogation' is like toddler-talk for grown-ups. Instead of just writing down facts and figures, turn things into questions. So, for instance, learning about 1066 and the Battle of Hastings might turn into a series of questions:

- Why did the Battle of Hastings take place in 1066?
- Did William really have the greater claim to the throne?
- What role did bluff play in luring Harold's forces into battle?

143

- What strategies were employed by William the Conqueror and King Harold? Why did they work for William and not for Harold?
- What difference did the Battle of Hastings make to the lives of people in England?
- What were the long-term consequences for the way England was governed?

Just shifting things like this makes your brain look at the information more in-depth and gets it more involved thinking about it. It's a form of testing and you know how good testing is!

When you're studying, ask yourself, 'what does this mean to me?' Form an opinion. Remember, you store information that has personal meaning more easily than information that doesn't.

Have a problem list...

If things keep tripping you up, make a list of these subjects. It gives you a problem-child set of topics to talk over with tutors or peers. Don't spend too long worrying about them, just set them aside until you can get help with them.

Making it happen

Some of these techniques will naturally fit your personal style and just 'click'. Others won't feel right, so bin them. As long as you're using techniques that work for you and not just falling into the old traps of writing out entire textbooks and hoping for the best, you'll get the results.

It's been said a couple of times – try speaking out loud as you work. You'll engage more than one part of the brain.

Get hands-on, write on paper, draw pictures – the more

bits of your brain you get involved, the better your chances of recall.

Whichever approach you use, make sure you're doing it consciously. Stop, think... don't let it become passive or you won't activate the networks. And remember, you need to reactivate the memory multiple times for it to stick – so get on it.

'Too long; didn't read' summary

- Start by honestly assessing your knowledge in different areas. Grade yourself with 'A', 'B', or 'C' according to how confident you feel answering questions on different exam topics.
- Don't neglect your 'A' areas – the fluency illusion means you can overestimate the depth of your knowledge if something feels familiar.
- Break up your revision and start early. Don't treat study as a 'reading phase' and a 'revision phase' – overlap them. It'll help reinforcement.
- Schedule revision time early. You don't want to run out of time or neglect it.
- Understanding is everything. Could you explain the issue or topic to a young child? If not, it could be you don't fully understand it yourself.
- Use a range of revision techniques. Mix it up and find the ones that work best for you. There are 12 outlined for you to choose from.
- Of all the techniques, don't neglect testing. This has been shown to be a hugely powerful revision technique so it's worth spending time on and there are different ways to use it.

4. Taming the beast

Chapter 9

Exam day preparations

"Chance favours the prepared mind" Louis Pasteur
"I'm not prepared. I really am not prepared at all. This is a surprise, I'll tell you" – Will Ferrel, Anchorman

What's in this chapter?

IT'S NEARLY EXAM DAY, so you need to look at the important steps you can take in the run up to your exam. Things to make sure you arrive on exam day feeling good and ready to go. You'll want to look at the importance of sleep, how to calm your exam nerves, and the all-important preparation for the day itself.

Cramming? Not ideal!

Let's tackle the big one straight away. Does 'cramming' for an exam work? Can you stay up the whole night before the exam, walk in there and blitz it?

Well, the answer is a rather frustrating, 'maybe', but it depends on different things.

Firstly, your own ability to concentrate for long periods of time. Not everybody can sit down for the 'all-nighters' some students routinely pull-off. Their brain simply won't play ball for that length of time. For others, cramming helps with their 'flow' state [1].

Secondly, since most people tend to cram the night before the exam, it depends on your relationship with sleep. There's more detail on this shortly, but you've already seen that sleep's essential for the functioning of the human body and memory. So, depriving yourself of sleep just before the exam often isn't good news.

And the big one (the real clincher, if you like), is that it depends on what you're trying to achieve. If all you want to do is pass the exam, you might be able to cram enough information into your head to get through it; you just won't remember that information in the long term. In chapter one you looked at how the memory works, and about the importance of periodic reinforcement to prevent forgetting. You also read about the difference between your ability to understand, and your ability to remember (chapter three).

When cramming for an exam, what you're reviewing is likely to make sense. It will probably 'go in' (at least in the short-term). But it's highly unlikely you'll be able to recall it again in the future. In other words, what you cram will be here today, gone shortly after the exam tomorrow. If you want to retain information past the exam, spaced learning is absolutely the better approach [2].

For some people, cramming's acceptable. They have no desire to retain knowledge for longer than it takes to pass the exam. But doesn't that make the exercise of taking the exam a bit pointless? You invest all your time and effort into getting a piece of paper with the word 'pass' on it, and not much more.

Instead, using the study and revision techniques outlined in this book will not only deliver you to the exam with the knowledge in your head, but you'll also have the ability to keep it there in the longer term.

So, it isn't that cramming doesn't work. I'd be lying if I said it didn't. I've used it myself, when I really needed to, and I've got through the exams. But I honestly couldn't tell you anything about those subjects now. In fact, a staggering 40% of British students would fail an exam they'd previously passed, if asked to take it again a year later [3]. So, while research has shown cramming 'can' work, it only works in the short term [4,5].

That said, if you are going to cram, at least do it right.

If you've taken nothing else from this book so far, you hopefully realise need to use your time wisely when you're studying. If you've only got a limited amount of time available to cram, sitting down with the book and reading it over-and-over again won't to work (see chapter five). So, how can you make the most of your cramming?

1. Choose your subjects

If you've reached the point where cramming's needed, you're in the departure lounge at 'Last Chance International Airport'. There's absolutely no time for any kind of junk study here (chapter three). If you don't need it for the exam, you can't afford to be cramming it. At this stage, your priority areas really are your priority areas – concentrate on the big rocks and getting them solidly in place.

Go back to your original schedule and the syllabus; be honest with yourself. What do you need to work on if you're going to have a chance of getting through this?

As a reminder, beware the 'fluency illusion' (chapter eight). Sometimes you trick yourself into thinking you know certain

151

subjects but, when you scratch beneath the surface, you find you don't know as much as you think. Which leads you to...

2. *Test, test, test*

Testing is the super-technique for revision (chapter eight), and when it comes to cramming, that still holds true. If you want to get information into your head in short-order, crack open those past papers, form a crammers' circle with your friends and ask each other questions. Make your cramming active rather than passive. By testing yourself, and other people, you're challenging your brain to tackle the information in a completely different way.

3. *Mix it up*

Don't just sit and read the book. Use the techniques outlined in chapter eight to mix up your approach to the material. Try some flashcards, take a walk through your memory palace, draw out pictures, write a song – whatever works for you. Keep it varied, keep it interesting.

4. *Do more than one session*

Assuming you've not arrived on exam night and found yourself looking at this book for inspiration (let's hope not, for all our sakes), try to space out your cramming sessions over two nights (or even three) rather than just one. You'll spend less time cramming per night, be able to get more sleep, and let you reinforce your learning.

The week before the exam

OK, so for the rest of this chapter, let's move beyond the issue of cramming and think about more practical aspects. Either you've followed the guidance elsewhere in the book and have done your revision in advance, or you'll now have the best approach to cramming.

Either way, there are things you'll need to do if you're going to make the exam experience as painless as possible. The process of tackling the exam itself is in chapters ten and eleven, so here you'll look at everything else that makes for a successful exam-day experience.

In the week before the exam, your focus should be on two things:

1. Final revision – tidying up and refining those last subjects, and
2. Getting prepared for exam day.

You need to make sure you've got everything you need – will you need ID at the exam centre? Is there an admission permit? If you're taking the exam online, do you have the right software and hardware? Will you have any firewall problems? (That's often an issue if you're using a company computer). Get those checks done nice and early with plenty of time to get issues resolved.

The key to this preparation focuses on three issues: "What, when, and how?" Make sure you have them covered!

The day before the exam

If you've done your preparation and you're not cramming, the day before the exam is a time to relax.

That might sound daft, but it really isn't. The more relaxed you are on exam day, the better your chances. So, do something else – something you enjoy. Maybe watch TV, go to the gym, or go for dinner with your family. Basically, anything that isn't exam focused. Give your brain time to get itself ready (and it does that best if you let it chill out with some pleasant down time).

Now, experience tells me students just can't bring themselves to step totally away from the books the day before an exam, so let's have a compromise. Spend an hour or two (at most) reviewing your revision. (Remember, testing is the most powerful approach – use your flashcards, your Cornell notes, or even just review mock questions). Doing that will make you feel you've given it your all. And then, step back.

You know stress negatively impacts on retrieval of memories [6], so focusing on anything that helps get you into a positive headspace and keep calm is a winner.

Exam day

There's a common saying amongst runners, "Nothing new on race day". It means that the day of a race is not the time to be trying out new shoes. They might look great, but best to stick with what you know if you don't want to end up with blisters. Exams work in a similar way. The day of the exam is not the time to reinvent the wheel.

You want to arrive at the exam feeling calm, prepared, and ready to go. So here are my go-to tips which I've found really helpful over the years:

1. Eat!

The brain runs on the same thing as your muscles – glyco-gen. If you've ever done a workout and found there's just nothing left in the tank, it's often because you've not fuelled properly. You need to eat before an exam, even if you don't have much. Fuel the brain for the workout you're about to give it.

2. Get there early

There's nothing more guaranteed to bring about stress than sitting in traffic, or waiting for a late train, when the start of the exam is inching ever closer. Plan your journey so you arrive in plenty of time. Sometimes exams are held in rooms that aren't all that easy to find – give yourself the time you need, and you'll be a lot less flustered.

If you're taking your exam online at home, do the set-up early. Check your equipment.

If it's going to be remotely invigilated (rather than open book) make sure there's nothing around that might cause your invigilator concern. Take down the study wall notes if they're in the same room – they aren't going to take too kindly to those being in your eyeline come start time!

3. Try to keep yourself to yourself

They say misery loves company. Sadly, it is true. People who feel bad about themselves and their situation want to feel they're not alone in their discomfort, so they often try to bring other people into their misery. It isn't uncommon for students outside exam halls to steadily drive each other down into a spiral of despair.

One person talks about a subject they've decided is 'definitely coming up', another realises they've not studied that subject in much depth and starts to panic. To bring company to their misery, they try to find the 'golden bullet' topic they've studied that other students haven't. They hit upon one, and the other person starts to panic. Now both are in a state, and neither has any idea what's in the paper yet!

Instead, avoid the 'pre-mortem' discussions and try to keep some distance from other people. Mentally prepare yourself in your own way.

While we're on this subject – be careful when you come out too. Often, people try to make themselves feel better about their perceived failure by pulling others down. The only person who knows whether you answered correctly, is the person who marks your paper, so why waste energy talking about it?

4. Listen to music

If you've read all the chapters so far, you'll already know about the power of music as a memory aid (chapters one, six and eight). If you've followed the advice and used a 'trigger song', now is the time to take out your headphones (or buds) and get it playing. Play it a couple of times. Take yourself back to the feeling of listening to that song in your study sessions, recreate the scene... really immerse yourself in the feeling.

It might sound odd but doing this will fire up those neural networks and kickstarts your brain, sending it on the hunt for the exam-related material.

Even if you've not been using the trigger-song technique, music is still good. Ever watched the Olympics? When the swimmers come out to the pool, or the athletes come out to the track, how many of them are wearing headphones? Pretty much all of them. Music is incredibly powerful for grounding us and preparing us for the challenges ahead (It's also really helpful for keeping you out of the 'pre-mortem' discussions, #winning).

Pick music you find calming. You might be someone who listens to thrash metal and feels blissfully chilled. (Personally, I'd find that a bit like chewing cotton wool!) Or maybe you'd prefer some chilled guitar tracks (try Jose Gonzalez – that's always guaranteed to make me feel better, more positive, and ready to go). Whatever your choice, find it and use it!

5. Breathe!

I once saw David Beckham telling his favourite joke about himself. It went broadly along the following lines: David Beckham is sat in his hairdresser's chair with his headphones on. The hairdresser accidentally knocks the headphones to the floor, and, in a panic, Beckham starts gasping for breath. His face goes red, then purple. He dives to the floor, picks up the headphones, puts them back on and hears, 'breathe in, breathe out.'.

I like that joke, but this isn't about reminding you to breathe (you're smart, you understand the benefits of breathing). What you do need to do, is breathe with purpose. Take deep breaths in through your nose, and out through your mouth. Concentrating on the feeling of that breath, puts you in a more mindful state, and increases your feelings of calm.

You'll read more about handling exam nerves shortly, but even confident exam takers can benefit from being more mindful. The research on the benefits of mindfulness is vast and it all agrees – being mindful is good news for your mental state. Just taking a little time outside the exam to do some deep breathing and concentrate your mind will pay dividends when you get into the exam hall.

. . .

6. Go over your notes for a few minutes – use key words
Spend just a few minutes going over your notes. Again, this starts the process of firing up your neural networks. Don't try to read lengthy passages, just revisit your key words (Cornell note system or flashcards) and ask yourself questions. You'll have a kick-start before you even get into the exam.

Calming exam nerves

Much of this chapter is about calming your nerves and getting you in the best mental state for the exam but, for some people, exam nerves are a major problem. If you're one of these students, your nerves extend well beyond the normal range of 'butterflies in the tummy' and closer toward 'stone-cold terror'.

One of the big problems with extreme nerves is that if you're nervous while you're thinking about the exam, you're using part of your working memory. That limits your ability to bring in other memories. It's an incredibly difficult situation and you have my sincere sympathies.

While there isn't scope in a book like this to go into depth on the many ways to try and overcome problem stress, there are some things which other students have found useful, and some resources you can look at, both of which might help.

Before getting into that, let's think about what you're really feeling. When you feel those exam nerves, what's going on? Well, your body's an incredibly sophisticated system, designed to protect you from threats. In the days of our ancestors, we weren't the apex predators we are today – in fact, we were likely to end up as dinner if we weren't careful. So, to stop us from featuring on the menu of the friendly neighbourhood tiger, our bodies developed our 'fight, flight, or freeze' system.

When confronted with a threat, those three things cover most of your options – you can stand up and fight it, you can run away from it, or you can freeze and hope it doesn't notice you. To prepare for the first two, your brain needs to get in gear, and it all starts with a part of the brain known as the amygdala.

This part of the more primal brain handles your emotions. It picks up that something's going on and starts a chain of events leading to the release of stress hormones – cortisol and adrenaline – to prepare the body for whatever comes next. These hormones are incredibly useful if you need to run like the wind or stand and face down a tiger. But, when they're triggered too often, and with no obvious 'enemy', they can seriously damage your health and wellbeing.

Small amounts of stress can be good. Cortisol stimulates the release of dopamine which helps memory (chapter one) but too much is dangerous. Over time it can actually damage the ability of your hippocampus to file new memories and can prevent proper recall of old ones.

Thankfully, the effect can be reversed.

In the modern world, 'threats' have changed. The closest you're likely to get to an angry cat is your own moggy playing up because you didn't feed it early enough. But your body hasn't evolved at the same pace as society and your internal systems for threat protection are the same as they were.

That's why, when your body senses a threat – in this case, an exam – it floods you with stress hormones. Your heart rate starts to race, you get butterflies in your tummy, and you have that horrible feeling of dread hanging over you. The good news, though, is that if you recognise it for what it is – your body trying to be helpful – you can start to work on it and use it to your advantage.

One simple technique I've used with lots of nervous exam takers is called 'anchoring' – a simple form of mindfulness training. Mindfulness and meditation are clinically proven to enhance health and lower stress, so they're perfect for exams. This exercise takes around ten minutes a day in the week running up to the exam and it's all about breathing.

All you do, is sit somewhere you won't be disturbed. Get comfortable, close your eyes, and start to breathe deeply. Breathe in through your nose and out through your mouth. Concentrate on the feeling of the breath. After a minute or two you should start to feel more relaxed. As you continue to breathe in through your nose and out through your mouth, just squeeze together the thumb and forefinger on whichever hand you don't use for writing.

Do this for around ten minutes, then come back to the world and get on with your day. You'll feel calmer, should be refreshed and, importantly, you'll have started the process of linking those feelings to the 'anchor' of squeezing your fingers together.

On exam day, if you start to feel the panic setting in, recognise it's just your body helping you. Start the deep breathing and squeeze your fingers together in the 'anchor'. You should find you start to calm quickly.

If you want to explore mindfulness in more depth, there are various apps you can download which offer guided meditations from a few minutes to an hour ('Balance', 'Calm', and many more). Most of them offer a free trial, so download one and give it a try.

Some other things you might try to help with exam nerves include:

- **Exercise** – You've seen already how powerful exercise can be for memory, but it also helps control stress. Even light exercise can be very beneficial.

- **Write about how you feel** – This might sound a little 'out there', but the action of writing down how you feel forces the brain to process it differently and can result in lower levels of anxiety. Write yourself a letter, as if you were telling a close friend how you feel. Then, re-read it and consider the advice you'd give someone else if they'd sent that letter to you. You'll be amazed at the effect.
- **Smile** – Just smiling reduces stress. The body is all wired together, and smiling's a powerful signal that the world isn't as bad as you feared. Watch some good comedy, or just talk to someone who lifts your spirits.
- **Ease off on the caffeine** – Caffeine can significantly increase your anxiety levels. Back off on the caffeinated drinks in the run-up to the exam if you want to keep your nerves under control.
- **Know your own signals and respond** – Sometimes, just knowing yourself and your early signals is enough. Recognise your early signs of stress and jump on them before they get a grip.
- **Kill the ANTs** – Everyone has ANTs (Automatic Negative Thoughts). These are the little mental notes you send yourself to keep yourself down. "I'm terrible at exams", "I'm not as bright as the others". When you feel these ANTs scurrying around, stamp on them. Talk to yourself as you'd talk to a close friend and be kind to yourself [7].

The importance of sleep

One of the most problematic results of pre-exam stress is its impact on sleep. It can become a vicious circle: nerves lead to poor sleep, poor sleep leads to more stress, more stress leads to worse sleep [8]. The exercises outlined above can help to break this cycle, but it's also worth thinking about sleep in a more general sense.

The restorative effects of sleep are well documented. Anyone who's raised children (or even shared a house with a baby) will know the impact poor sleep can have. The strange thing is nobody really knows why we sleep. What we do know is there are clear physiological benefits to sleep, many of which will help in exam taking. These include:

1. **Memory consolidation** – when you sleep, you reinforce and back up your memories (chapter one). The fact that so many students decide to exchange sleep for cramming is clearly not helpful in this context [9].
2. **Energy conservation** – sleep is a period of 'downtime' so your body can conserve its energy for the day to come. This is especially important before exams when you're putting yourself through stress.
3. **Immune function** – poor sleep impairs the operation of your immune system. Nobody wants to hit exam day with a streaming nose or a sore throat.

Various researchers have shown poor sleep leads to poor exam performance – both when it's the night before the exam, and in the run-up to the exam. Bottom line? Make sure you're getting your sleep if you want to perform on exam day.

'Too long; didn't read' summary

- Although 'cramming' can be effective, it only works for short-term retention. You'll likely forget everything you've crammed shortly after the exam's complete.
- If you do cram, do it with purpose. Don't just read the book. Mix up your techniques and use plenty of testing – either of yourself, others, or both!
- Plan ahead. The week before the exam, think about the practicalities – where's it taking place, when is it, how will you get there, what will you need etc.?
- The day before the exam, try to do something other than study (unless you're cramming, of course). Relaxation and down time put your brain in the best state for exam day.
- On the day, get there early, and try to keep to yourself a little. Listening to other people often causes stress, so avoid thinking "but I didn't revise that!"
- Exam nerves are very common. Your body doesn't know the difference between a real threat and a perceived one. Invest time in techniques like 'anchoring' in the run-up to the exam, to help keep you calm on exam day.

Chapter 10

Tackling written exams

"There is nothing to writing. All you do is sit down at a type-writer and bleed." Ernest Hemingway
"The scariest moment is always just before you start." Stephen King

What's in this chapter?

IN THIS CHAPTER, you'll cover the essential techniques for tackling a written exam. You'll look at the importance of reading the exam paper before you get started, the order you should tackle the questions and the format and depth of your answers. You'll also learn the importance of keeping on top of time.

There's a method...

You've done the work. You've learned the material and you've spent time locking that material in your head. All is good; you're ready.

Whether you pass is now just a matter of two things – how you handle your mindset, and how you show the examiner your wares. You've already looked at how to tackle your nerves (chapter nine), which just leaves technique – and what a big one that is!

So many students go into the exam with all the knowledge but end up losing out due to poor technique. My aim here is to give you what you need to make sure you're not one of them.

Read the whole paper

The first thing you need to do when tackling a written paper, is read it. All of it. Spend time reading through all the questions you're need to answer and make rough notes for each of them. These notes will act as your 'quick win marks' when you start writing.

This might feel like wasted time but there is good science behind it, and once again it relates primarily to the way your brain works.

Let's step away from the computer metaphor for the brain and instead imagine your memory as an enormous filing cabinet. You saw in chapter one how much storage space it has, so that cabinet's going to be vast. Picture it as four drawers high, and three miles long. Some of the information is right next to you, in the nearest drawers. Other information is right down at the far end - it's quite a journey to go and retrieve it.

When you read the entire paper through, you start the process of looking for the information. If some of that information is stored elsewhere, you can send your internal administrator on a run to the far end of the cabinet. Meanwhile, you can crack on with the questions for which you can easily access answers. By the time you've done those ones, and you reach the tricky one, your mental admin will be back waiting for you with all the information you need, neatly packaged in a file (well, hopefully).

This isn't new. We all experience this in our day-to-day lives. You chat to your friends, and you get talking about that actor, "You know, the one who played Spiderman. No, not Tom Holland, earlier, dated Kirsten Dunst. No? Oh, it doesn't matter". The conversation moves on. Then, about half an hour later, while you're chatting about something totally different, you blurt out, "Tobey Maguire!".

Reading your paper upfront gives you the best chance that the 'Tobey Maguire moment' will come while you're still in the exam hall, and not in the car on the way home.

What's the alternative? Well, you could just dive straight into the paper without reading it all first. You might find the answers to questions one and two come easily. Unfortunately, when you get to question three and discover you don't have the information to hand, you're now short on time and the mental admin doesn't have time to get there and back before the end of the exam. So, there's no harm in reading everything first, right?

The order you answer

Once you've read the paper from start to finish, you should be ready to start tackling the questions. The next issue is the order in which you answer them.

This is one where you need to find out before the exam. Check what your exam board requires, and allows, as part of your research before you start studying (chapter two). Some will insist you tackle the questions in the order they're presented, although in my experience that's quite rare.

Most allow you to answer them in any order you like but ask you to complete sub-parts together. So, for instance, if you're tackling question 1, and it's split into parts a, b, and c, you need to do all three parts together, and then choose the next question.

Assuming you're allowed to approach them in whatever order you like, get some easy wins by taking on the question you're most confident about first. Leave the one where you're least confident until last.

Remember, having read the entire question paper upfront, your subconscious mind is now plugging away in the background, working through the answers to the later questions. Meanwhile you're busy smashing the earlier ones out of the park.

Answer the question they asked

I've got bad news for you – answering the question you wish the exam board was asking, rather than the one they're actually asking you, isn't going to get you far in most cases. Believe me, I know. It's really frustrating.

1993, my A-Level year and I was studying History. I'd prepped the backside out of the Russian Revolution. I knew it inside and out, up-and-down. I was all over it. Each year for over a decade, there'd been two questions on that subject, and I intended to answer them both.

This year they decided not to ask about it – at all. Of course, I could have tried to twist the questions they asked to show how much I knew about Russia, but I'd have got no marks for it. The examiner may have tipped their virtual cap to me, but that doesn't get you an A-Level. Instead, I had to answer the question they did ask and that meant moving right down the line to my reserve subject.

(Incidentally, true story... my mum used to work at a school. The night before my history exam she brought home a book she'd picked up at a library clear-out. The book was about the

League of Nations. She asked if it was any good to me. I gave it a look through 'just in case'. Guess what I ended up answering a question on? How's that for fate!)

Beyond just answering the question posed, make sure you're answering the *specific* question they've asked. Before you dive into your answer, make sure you know exactly what's required. If the question asks you to critically assess, you won't get many marks for just explaining.

Look for keywords and the 'action verb'. Are you being asked to 'describe', 'explain', 'analyse', or just 'list'? If you're using a physical exam paper, circle the verb. If it's online, write it down on your rough paper.

There's a caveat here. In some exams you can get a pass, albeit not a high pass, for giving an excellent answer to a related question. If you really can't answer the question that's been set, and your exam happens to have this option, there is potential merit in telling the examiner what you know. If, however, like most exams, there are no marks for related, but not relevant information, you might as well devote the time to other questions instead. Who knows, by the time you've done all the others, you might be able to find a few marks for the tough one from the depths of your memory banks.

Get your depth right

One of the most common problems in exams is what's affectionately call 'brain-dumping'. This simply means writing far too much about a subject; downloading everything you know onto the page. It tends to happen for two reasons:

1. You've learned lots of good stuff and you want to show how much you've learned.

2. You haven't properly understood what you've studied, so you're throwing everything but the kitchen sink at the examiner and hoping for the best.

Unfortunately, brain dumping isn't the right approach. Everyone wants to show how much they know, but if there are no marks for it, leave it out. It doesn't matter how much you tell the examiner; nothing is going to get you 20 marks for a 3-mark question. You're better off being smart with your time. If there are three marks, limit your answer to the relevant stuff and accept you've carried lots of extra stuff around in your head for no marks. It happens. And it's all knowledge for the future.

The second reason is tougher, because the solution lies before the exam. Chapter six talked a lot about taking good notes and that you should never write down something you don't understand. This is why it's so important. If you make sure you understand your material as you're studying it, you shouldn't be left in this situation on exam day. You'll be better placed to work out which is the most important information and how to adapt your knowledge to the needs of the question.

Consider your format

I've marked many exam papers over the years, and it never ceases to amaze me how many students don't follow the examiner's instructions for the format of their answers. Quite often, the examiner will include a statement like:

"Unless otherwise called for, give your answers in bullet points or brief paragraphs"

Despite this, students give lengthy prosaic answers, which waste their own time and make it harder to mark.

To show you what this feels like to the examiner, here's an

example. Look at the following question, then consider the two versions of the answer underneath:

"Briefly outline the five stages of team development in the expanded Tuckman model" (5 marks)

Option A

The Tuckman model of team development was formulated by psychologist Bruce Tuckman in 1965 and outlined in his paper "Developmental Sequence in Small Groups". It sets out the stages that a team passes through as it comes together and performs its tasks.

Originally, Tuckman outlined four stages, but a fifth stage has since been added – 'adjourn' – recognising that many teams come together for a specific purpose and then disband when the team has completed its goal.

To begin with, individuals are assembled with a goal in mind. In stage one, they 'form' a notional team, but they operate more as individuals because they've not yet developed a group identity. Trust is likely to be lacking at this stage and this lack of trust continues into the next stage – 'storming'. Here, everyone is trying to find where they belong and the 'pecking order' is being established. There are likely to be clashes between team members and the leader's authority may be challenged. Individual team members can end up feeling overwhelmed if the boundaries and expectations aren't clearly defined.

The third stage is 'norming'. At this point, the team members settle their differences, and they all settle into their role. The leader's authority becomes respected, and the team develops stronger bonds. At this point they're operating more as a team and less as individuals. This leads to the fourth stage, 'performing', where the team operates at its optimum level and gets things done. Everyone knows their role, and everyone contributes.

Option B

- Forming – In the early stage, people come together to start a project, but there's no group cohesion. People act as individuals, not team members.
- Storming – people find their place. Boundaries are pushed and there can be clashes between members. If responsibilities aren't clear, team members can be overwhelmed.
- Norming – conflicts are resolved, people settle into their role, and the leader's authority is respected. Team bonds become stronger.
- Performing – the team works at full potential and productivity is high. Setbacks can cause movement back to earlier stages.
- Adjourning – having completed the task, the group disbands

Both answers get to the information the examiner wants, and both would likely score full marks. But the first takes considerably longer to write, contains lots of information that isn't relevant to the question and won't pick up marks, and is harder for the examiner to mark. The fact that the stages aren't given in fully sequential order – adjourn coming before the others – also means the examiner can't just work down the list and award a mark for each.

If the question calls for an essay, give them one, otherwise give them the format they want – usually bullets. Either way, know what's being asked of you, and deliver it.

Your answers should almost challenge the examiner to give you marks. If the question's worth 10 marks, your bullet points should each stand up and say to the examiner – "this is worth a mark, tell me it isn't!"

You do need to be slightly careful though. On examples like the above, the five marks translate easily into the five stages of the model, so it's easy to see where the marks come from. In some cases, it will be less clear, or you might be able to think of more options than there are marks. Don't be afraid to include a little more than you have to – just don't brain dump. So, to give a silly example, if there were 20 marks for naming all the Premier League teams from the 2020-21 season, but you couldn't remember whether Norwich were yo-yoing up or down that year, you might put 21 or 22 teams down. As long as the exam isn't negatively marked (where you lose marks for wrong information) there's no harm.

Format of essay

If the format of the question does require an essay, make sure there's a logical flow to it. The art of writing essays is covered in chapter seven and, if your exam might require one, it would be worth reviewing.

At the very least, you should make sure there's a clear structure with an introduction, an argument, support for that argument, and a conclusion.

If you find you're running out of time and can't write everything, at least finish off your sections using bullet points, although it's often worth leaving a note for the examiner to explain you've done that because time was short.

Clarity is key

One of the most frustrating things for a marker is not being able to award marks because you just can't understand what you're being told. This is particularly problematic in written exams. Students sacrifice handwriting quality for speed, thinking the more they write, the more marks they'll pick up. Of course, you already know it doesn't work this way, and if they can't read your writing, they can't give you any marks at all. So slow down and write clearly. Don't pretend to be a GP (seriously, do they run classes at medical school on how to make your writing indecipherable?)

Even if you're typing your answers, you still need to make sure they're clear. Keep a good structure, use the bullet points approach where possible and write in plain English if you can.

One final note here relates to calculations. This won't be the first time you've heard this, but please, please, please show your workings. When you're marking an exam paper and all you've been given is a wrong answer, you can't award any marks at all. If you're marking the same paper and you've been given all the workings, often the examiner can see where the mistake has been made and can give credit for the other steps in the process. Make it clear, lay out your workings in a logical order, and help the examiner to help you.

Application

Repeating stuff you've read in past exam papers, without applying it to the question you've been asked isn't going to get you far! You have been warned.

To pick up the marks, you need to know your material and be able to apply it, which means you need to understand it. Repetition might cut it at GCSE, but at any other level, you need to be able to manipulate the information and apply it to the scenario in front of you. And really understanding something means being able to explain it to someone else (Feynman's notebook in chapter eight, remember?).

If you can make it simple to understand, you must understand it at a deeper level yourself.

It's also worth, wherever possible, relating your answer to the question. If the question involves a particular person, refer to their name in your answer and explain how your answer impacts them, rather than just giving a generic response.

Don't keep stuff in working memory

Often, students (especially when they've crammed) will go into the exam with lots of information stored in their working memory. Remember, you've only got a very limited capacity for this part of your memory, and you need that capacity to answer the question in hand. Information needs to be called up from your long-term memory (your cloud) and opened in the working memory (the desktop) during the exam.

If the desktop is cluttered with notes of formulae or references, you won't have room for the things you need. So, purge!

As soon as you're told you can start, write down anything you've tried to keep in short-term working memory on your rough paper. Now you don't need to hang on to it and you can focus on answering the questions.

Leave space and let it brew

Chapter seven talked about a core strategy – called 'incubation' - for solving tough problems in coursework and essays. In simple terms, it's about leaving something well alone and letting it float around in your mind. More often than not, your brain will come up with a solution.

It works much like the filing cabinet analogy from earlier. You ask the brain a question and, just as it can go searching in the files to find the answer, it can also work creatively to find one.

When talking about this for coursework, I suggested stepping away from your desk and doing something completely different – taking the dogs for a walk or sitting in the garden. Of course, that's not really an option in the exam, but you can still take time out. If a question's troubling you, park it. Leave your brain to ponder and come back to it later. It might be you didn't have as much knowledge to hand as you thought and you'll need to plunder your database, or you might need the creative element of your brain to form a project group, run some meetings, and generate a report! Either way, the brain can do this without your conscious involvement, so let it.

Keep honest on time

"Time and tide wait for no man" said Chaucer (although I prefer, "Time and tide melts the snowman" which comes from Dr Who). Either way, keep track of time or face the consequences.

You might remember reading about the 'flow' state and our friend Mihali Csikszentmihalyi (usual spelling!) in chapter three. This is a state in which you become absorbed by a task that's just about at the edge of your ability. Too easy and you get bored, too hard and you become frustrated, but just right and you're like Goldilocks with a bowl of lukewarm porridge. When you're in the flow state, you lose track of time, you get swept along by the task and what feels like a minute turns out to be an hour.

While flow can result in some wonderful answers to exam questions, it also risks causing you to run out of time if you're not very careful, and that can be very bad news. Becoming engrossed in a 15-mark question is great, but if the exam's only one-hour long and there are 60 marks, you can't afford to spend too much time on that one question, otherwise the later ones aren't getting answered.

My top tip here is to know how long you have for each mark, divide your time accordingly, and make sure you hit certain checkpoints along the way.

So, imagine you're facing a three-hour exam and there are 150 marks up for grabs. Allow 15 minutes to read through the entire paper and make rough notes. During that time, decide on the order you're going to tackle the questions. Then allocate one minute per mark, which leaves you 15 minutes at the end for a sweep-up.

If your first question is worth 15 marks, you will want to be moving on to the next one 15 minutes after you start writing. To keep yourself focused, when you write out the order you intend to tackle the questions, put a rough time against each one (the time you expect to start that question). If you find you're slipping against those timings, you know you need to pick it up a bit. You can always go back to questions at the end if there's time.

This might sound like a basic point, but these are often the ones that make the difference between passing and failing.

I remember once marking a student's paper. The exam called for them to answer five out of six possible questions. The first four answers were exceptional. Some of the best work I've seen. Unfortunately, there was no fifth answer. Just a note of apology that the student had run out of time. Doh!

'Too long; didn't read' summary

- Passing written exams is one part knowledge and one part method. Good exam technique will amplify the effects of your study.
- Start by reading the whole paper and making rough notes. This allows your subconscious mind to start looking for answers to the trickier questions, while your conscious mind works on the rest.
- Unless you're required to answer the questions in a set order, start with the ones you're most confident about and work down to the ones where you're less confident.
- Answer the question you've been asked, not the one you wish you'd been asked! No matter how much you might want to show your knowledge, you won't get 20 marks for a 3-mark question, so stop writing.
- Format is key. Challenge the examiner to give you marks by writing in bullet points wherever possible. Keep your answers clear and, if handwriting, legible. Show your workings.
- If you're struggling with a question, leave it and come back later. The process of 'incubation' often results in your brain generating creative answers.
- Keep track of time. Many students fail simply because time gets away from them. Have a rough idea how many minutes you have per mark (or how many marks per minute) and try to set checkpoints throughout the exam.

Chapter 11

Tackling multiple choice exams

"When given too many choices, people tend to worry that there's something better out there than what they decided on" Fumio Susaki
"I want that one..." Little Britain

What's in this chapter?

NOT ALL EXAMS REQUIRE ESSAYS. That's why this chapter covers hints and tips for taking multiple choice exams. Knowing the format of the exam, keeping on track of time, and being aware of the way your brain makes snap decisions can all make the difference between a 'pass' and a 'fail'.

How hard can it be?

"It's just a 'multiple-guess' exam, Jon, how hard can it be?" This is what one of my students once said to me, shortly before spectacularly crashing-and-burning in his exam. The answer, it turns out, is 'really quite hard, actually!'

Way back in chapter two, there was a table which talked about the 'levelling' of an exam. If an exam's set at 'level 4', it's at the level you might expect for a first-year undergraduate exam at university, and they don't give those passes away, you know. You're going to be expected to know your stuff and apply it accurately. You certainly shouldn't underestimate the size of the task.

In fact, in some senses, multiple choice exams can actually be harder than written ones. With a written exam you've got the opportunity to show the examiner what you know in more creative ways. If you're not quite sure what they're looking for, you can come at it from multiple angles and give them a little more information to cover your bases. Not so with a multiple choice exam. Here, you either get the right answer, or you don't. It's that simple.

The good news is that even with multiple choice exams, there are still techniques and tips you can use to give yourself the best chance of passing. (I've seen many students over the years fail multiple choice exams by just one or two marks. Following the tips in this chapter could well have been enough to give them the extra couple they needed to pass, so it's worth spending a little time on).

What's the format?

The first thing you need to understand is what format the questions will take. The term 'multiple choice' can mean different things to different people, so it's important to make sure you're on the right page.

The main thing to know is whether you're getting 'old school' multiple choice questions, or the infuriating 'multiple response' questions often used in exams these days. (Yes, it matters...)

Questions in these types of exams all have common elements:

1. **A stem** – this sets out the question, or the problem you're being asked to address
2. **Alternatives / answers** – the options from which you need to select

Where the two forms of question diverge is in the second element. With traditional multiple choice questions, there's a single correct answer, with a number of 'distractors' (wrong answers). In most cases, you'll see three distractors alongside your correct answer.

The alternative form – multiple response – generally involves four or five options, but with more than one correct answer. The problem is you need to get all the correct answers to gain the single mark. So, if there are three correct options, and only one incorrect option, you need to select all three or you get nothing at all.

Why does this matter? Well, the second type are objectively harder. There's more opportunity for you to miss out on the mark. You might know for a fact that two of the options are correct, but if you're not sure about a third, it becomes 50/50!

Knowing the format of your exam is important as you prepare. If the exam involves multiple response questions, are all the questions be in that format, or just some of them? If only some, how many?

RT(F)Q

This is probably the most important piece of advice you'll ever get when it comes to multiple choice exams – 'Read The (Flippin') Question'. In an exam environment, it's likely you'll be a bit nervous and, as you saw in chapter nine, that can do strange things to your brain. Students often 'snatch' at questions – giving them a quick skim over, and then grabbing for the option that seems right.

It's normal. Time is a factor, and you can't afford to waste it. But equally you need to take time to read the question properly, to make sure you really understand what's being asked.

You'll remember from chapter five that 'speed reading' studies have found it's associated with lower levels of reading accuracy. The faster you read, the more chance you have of getting the wrong message – and, by extension, the wrong answer.

So, read the question. Then read it again, to make sure you read it properly the first time. Take your time on this, because there's nothing more important than making sure you know what you're being asked.

As you read, look for important words that give you a clue. In particular, look for 'absolutes':

- 'Always' means there can never be a situation where this isn't the case. If you can think of one, this can't be the right answer.
- 'Never' means the opposite – it cannot be the case in any situation. If you know of an instance where it would be, it isn't right.
- 'All' – self-explanatory – all of them must apply.
- 'None' – again, self-explanatory. If you can think of one that might not apply, that can't be the right option.

What do you want to see?

Once you've read the question a couple of times, wherever possible, don't look at the answers straight away. Instead, ask yourself, 'What do I want to see?' Try to answer the question without the benefit of the options. When you do that, you're interrogating the database of your brain at quite a sophisticated level. You're asking it to find the answer with no prompts.

If you come up with an answer, look at the options to see if any of them match what you were thinking. If they do, it's looking pretty good for that being right.

Strike out the obvious wrong'uns

Sometimes, the question will lend itself to working out what the right answer is going to be, and other times you just won't be able to. In these cases, try to eliminate the obviously wrong options. As Sherlock Holmes said, "If you eliminate the impossible, whatever is left, however improbable, must be the answer."

Writing multiple choice questions isn't easy and there are only so many plausible wrong answers an examiner can come up with. My own experience tells me there are likely to be one or two slightly less plausible 'distractors' thrown in there. If you can eliminate one possible answer, your odds improve from one-in-four, to one-in-three just by guessing. If you can eliminate more than one, even better.

Don't get hung up on words you don't understand

Some students waste so much time trying to work out what the different options mean. Sometimes, examiners word them in such a way it's like swimming through treacle.

Where it gets daft, though, is when students waste time trying to decipher possible options, having already established that one of the options is right!

Take this example: "Which of the following words means 'the acquisition of knowledge or skills through study or experience?'"

1. Onomatopoeia
2. Learning
3. Floccinaucinihilipilification
4. Sequestration

You might not know that option 'A' means a word that sounds like the thing it describes (buzz, for instance), that option 'C' means something without value, or that option 'D' is the Scottish version of bankruptcy. What you **do** know is that option 'B' means the acquisition of knowledge. So don't get hung up on the others. If you know option 'B' is the right one, select it and move on.

Gut feeling or head?

If you've read the Chimp Paradox by Steve Peters [1], you'll be familiar with the idea we have two different systems competing in our heads. If you're not familiar with it, here's a quick summary.

Your brain has the primal 'limbic system', responsible for the kind of behaviours that keep you alive – feeding, reproduction, etc. This sits deep inside the brain and is surrounded by the grey wrinkly bit, known as the cortex.

In the analogy used by Steve Peters, the limbic system is the 'chimp'. It makes snap decisions based on very little information. That's it's job. If a car is hurtling toward you, you want your brain to very quickly decide that moving out of the way is going to be the right answer.

The cortex is your 'human'. This is the part that makes calm, collected and more rational, decisions. Unfortunately, it's lazy and it quite happily sits on the sofa while the chimp runs the show.

Imagine you're sat at a set of traffic lights and the light turns to green. You're daydreaming and don't notice. The next thing you know, the person behind is beeping their horn and waving at you in a none-too-friendly manner. The chimp reaction is to wind down the window and start shouting back at them. Who do they think they are? The human, however, looks at things more rationally. Perhaps this person is in a rush? Maybe they're trying to get to the hospital. Maybe they're just having a really bad day and lashing out. Either way, there are 86,400 seconds in a day, why let this five-second episode ruin the other 86,395? Taking a moment, having a deep breath, and then responding, is the best way to switch from chimp to human.

How does this relate to exams? Well, your chimp brain is likely to snatch at answers and can send you down the wrong path. Look at the following questions and just give the first answer that comes into your head:

1. A bat and ball cost £55. If the bat is £50 more than the ball, how much does the ball cost?
2. How many of each animal did Moses take onto the Ark?
3. If the number of lilies on a pond doubles every day, and after 30 days the pond is entirely covered with lilies, how many days did it take for half the pond to be covered?

I've used these questions with lots of people over the years. Let's think about the answers:

1. Many people instinctively answer £5, but the answer is £2.50. If the ball cost £5, then the bat would be £50, which is only £45 more. With a ball costing £2.50 and a bat costing £52.50 there's a £50 difference.
2. Although the Bible talks about two of each animal, it was Noah who apparently built the ark (tell me you didn't just hear 'brother Noah built the ark?')
3. If the pond is covered after 30 days but the number of lilies doubles daily, it would have been half covered on day 29, not day 15 which is many people's answer.

In each case, the chimp reaction potentially takes you down the wrong path. The answer is to make sure you answer with the human, and that means waking it up. This is one of the reasons why it's so important to read the question twice.

Flagging and returning

In a paper exam, it's quite easy to leave a question and come back to it. You can flick backwards and forwards at will, so if an answer doesn't come to mind straight away, leave it for now, but take care to leave the space on your answer paper (I've seen students skip an answer but not leave the space. Before they know it, all their answers are out of line, and they've got a major recovery operation to get things back on track!)

With most online systems, you have the option to 'flag' a question and come back to it later. If you can, use this.

Remember how your brain is a bit like a massive filing

cabinet (chapter ten)? Often, the answer you're looking for is in a drawer down the other end of that cabinet and you need to despatch your internal administrator to go find it. Leaving a question to return to later gives your subconscious mind time to hunt for the relevant information. You'd be surprised how many times you return to the question later and find the answer's now obvious. All that's happened is your brain has returned from the other end of the cabinet and brought the answer in its hand.

Just one thing to think about - if you do flag a question to come back to, it's generally a good idea to put a 'placeholder' guess in there. If you've guessed and then run out of time, you've got a one-in-four chance (in most exams) of guessing the right answer. If you leave it blank and then run out of time, you've got a 100% chance of getting the wrong answer.

The only time I wouldn't put a placeholder is where the exam is negatively marked (you'd lose a mark for a wrong answer). These are quite rare, but if your exam works that way, in that case you're better to leave it blank.

Should you change your answer?

Often, students find they've got time left at the end of the exam and they start flicking back through their answers. The more they look, the more they start to second-guess themselves and they inevitably get to the point where they need to decide – should they stick with their original answer or 'twist' and change it.

Throughout this book I've drawn on research wherever possible, and I'm almost always in agreement with the research. On this question, though, research and I nearly had a falling out.

My own view, built over many years working with students,

is that you should generally stick with your original answer. I've seen many students change a right answer to a wrong answer.

Research, however, suggests you should change the answer. A team of researchers from Germany looked at past studies, and ran their own, concluding that, more often, students would change from wrong to right rather than the other way around [2].

So, how do I square this one away? Do I fall in line with the researchers, or continue to be a maverick? And what should you do?

Well, thankfully, with more digging, I don't think there's a discrepancy after all. The key is in the way the researchers worded their advice, "Students should be informed about the benefits of changing initial answers to multiple choice questions once, when in reasonable doubt about these answers". The key words here? '...reasonable doubt'.

If you review your answers and find you hadn't read the question properly, you'd not looked at all four options in sufficient detail, or simply that your brain has rummaged up some extra information with the passing of time which wasn't available to you before, then there's reasonable doubt and you should change. If, however, you're just worrying over it and trying to talk yourself around, you should probably stick. (I think that keeps both myself and the researchers on the same page!)

Is it 'C'?

There's an old wisdom that, if you genuinely don't know the answer, you should pick 'C'. The origin of this is unclear but having written literally thousands of multiple choice questions in my time, I can see some sense in it.

When you write a multiple choice question, you often need

to find a correct answer, and three wrong answers, or 'distractors'. Generally, the first distractor comes easily, and more often than not the second one's quite easy too. The third tends to be more difficult – there are only so many wrong options you can think of. As a result, the correct answer gets dropped into slot three, while the examiner ponders the remaining wrong answer.

I tested this, entirely unscientifically, by looking at 500 multiple choice questions I'd written. I did, indeed, find 'C' was the right answer more than any other option, and for the above reason.

But, before you get too excited, there's bad news. The chances are your multiple choice exam will be taken on a computer. If that's the case, the chances are the options will be randomised to prevent this bias.

When the examiner enters the options, the system generally shuffles all of them, so they don't appear in the same order, preventing any potential 'C' (or other letter) bias.

So, are there other options? Well, William Poundstone thinks so [3]. He spent time looking at tests across school, college, and professional sectors and believes he's found patterns you can exploit if your knowledge of the subject lets you down. (In other words, always use your brain first, but if that's missing in action and you're going to guess, these might help):

1. 'All of the above' and 'none of the above' – where one of these options is given, it's more likely to be correct. Poundstone found 52% of the time these were given as options, they were the right option.
2. Look at what you've answered for the last few and the next few. He found answers don't repeat consecutively very often. So, if question three is 'A'

and question five's also 'A', his view is question four is less likely to be.

3. Choose the longest answer. This one is widely used by students. If in doubt, go for the longest one! The argument is that the longer the answer, the harder it is to construct as a distractor. (My own experience suggests this can work, but examiners have also got wiser to it! I often put very wordy distractors in for just this reason, but then I'm cruel).

In the interests of full disclosure, the sample Poundstone used to complete this analysis wasn't huge, and I've not validated the ideas myself. However, if you're in a hole, they seem as sensible as any other route!

'Too long; didn't read' summary

- Multiple choice exams aren't the soft option that some people would have you believe them to be. Remember, exams are set at 'levels'. Sitting a level four exam, for instance, will be broadly equal in difficulty whether it's written or multiple choice.
- Find out the format for the exam. Will all the questions be traditional 'one-from-four' or will there be 'multiple response' questions where you need to get more than one correct answer to win the point.
- Will there be negative marking? Guesses give you a good chance of 'blagging' a mark, but not if you lose marks for wrong answers.
- Read the question – twice – and think what the answer might be. Then look at the options.
- If you don't see the answer you wanted, start by eliminating the obviously wrong answers.
- When you know one option is the right one, don't get too hung up on whether you understand the other options. If there's only one right answer, you've got it.
- Be wary of trusting your gut feeling too much – your 'chimp' is liable to send you down the wrong track.
- If you aren't sure about answers, come back to them.
- Despite popular opinion, if you don't know, the answer isn't always 'C'!

5. Pulling it all together

That's all folks

"Well done is better than well said." Benjamin Franklin
"And that's all I have to say about that..." Forrest Gump

And now, the end is near...

You're nearly at the end of your journey through study and exam technique. I've had a blast pulling this all together and I hope you've enjoyed reading it and you'll take away strategies to help you sail through your exams.

Before you go, I want to go right back to the start and remind you every hour you spend studying is an investment. It's time you're taking away from other things, and you owe it to yourself (and your PlayStation) to make your sacrifice worthwhile.

There is no 'right' way to study. Anyone who tells you their way is 'the' way is simply wrong. The science doesn't support that notion, at all. What's 'right' will vary from person to person, and you'll find out how to work best for your own mind by trying things out. That said, there's no doubt trying the tech-

197

niques outlined in this book is likely to be more effective than just reading and re-reading the textbook. Don't get me wrong, it's an option, but I'd strongly suggest it isn't the best one.

Results day

Before I close off, I want to touch on results day. I really hope that when you get your results, you see the grade or outcome you want. Maybe it's about wanting to get over the line, or maybe you're striving for top marks. Whatever your goal, I sincerely hope you get there. But, and there's always a but, the reality of life tells us the journey from A to B isn't always a straight line.

I've passed more exams than I can remember, but I've not passed every exam I've ever taken at the first time of asking. Sometimes, the cards don't just fall in your favour. It might sound odd to be talking about missing out in a book that's all about passing exams, but I want to send you a personal message:

If it doesn't go your way the first time, don't be disheartened. If you gave it your best, you could do no more.

Regroup, go again, and know it isn't a reflection of you. It's just one of those things that happens to us all from time to time.

If it helps, a few years ago, I was running the Great North Run half marathon in Newcastle. On one of the bridges we ran under, there was a sign that stuck in my memory, "Remember, your run is about more than your finish time, it is about everything it took to get you to the start line". Take the same message for your exams too. If it doesn't go your way, remind yourself of the work you put in and be proud of yourself. There's more to life than just the paper, and there's always tomorrow for the pass.

Final thoughts from other students

In the process of writing this book, I went out to my LinkedIn community and asked them a question.

"If you could give one piece of advice to people studying for exams right now, what would it be? What's the one nugget you've found super helpful in your own studies?"

Why? Because it's all very well hearing from my experience and research but hearing from fellow travellers on the exam path might also be helpful. What follows is some of their thoughts, it's interesting to note that many of these comments echo the thoughts I've outlined in the book:

- "Little and often works the best... 1 hour of study, maybe 6 days per week will achieve a lot more than a single day of study"
- "Mnemonics always worked well for me" (see chapter 8)

- "Have a study timetable, and revisit this often to keep you on track. Then on exam day treat it like a performance (especially for anyone who has ever done any amateur dramatics) you only have one show, nothing in your off stage life can come onto that stage, pure focus on what you have to do."
- "Mind mapping got me through my A-levels - visualising the key points for a given topic and how they related to each other on a single side of A4, then learning it off by heart"
- "Having a study buddy to keep you accountable and to discuss the complex stuff with."
- "I've always found concentrating on the holes in your knowledge helpful. Take some past papers before you start studying, see where your gaps are and concentrate your studies in those areas."
- "Sample paper, sample paper, sample paper"
- "Practice past papers over and over but understand why the incorrect answer is incorrect and if you don't then seek support to have it explained to you"
- "What worked for me study wise is 40 mins on 20 mins off."
- "Enjoy the time you spend studying (or try to!), because in the process of studying, you are honing your craft and becoming better at what you do."
- "Listening to it. Reading it is fine, but for me listening to it made it sink in better. Writing notes, saying it out loud, and even recording myself saying it and playing it back."
- "For me, it's memorising a lot of information by forming a new word. Each letter represents something else. Then write down the word at the start of the exam on rough paper, to use as a

reference point in the exam like a checklist to make sure you've covered all areas."

- "Tailor revision around an individual! How do they learn best? How can they fit revision into their lives? Which method of qualification suits them?"

- "Study the curriculum and the weighting of questions in each area...I'm all about being efficient with your study and you can end up wasting a lot of time trying to understand something that may only be worth a mark or two...if it's even covered!"

- "Always read any accompanying examiner's notes to practice exams, they will tell you where previous candidates went wrong so help you avoid any pitfalls!"

- "Believe in yourself. How you talk to yourself matters. If you are having a tough time understanding a concept, instead of saying I can't understand this, try saying I haven't figured this out yet."

- "There's a time to be super creative. For most of us, doing exams probably isn't that time ... stick to the plan, state the question, answer the question, reiterate the answer to the question. And don't panic - it's amazing what you can remember if you've put the graft in."

And one more, just because it's so true:

"On the darkest of revision days just remember - nobody expects you to get 100%! Perfection, while aspirational, is unlikely. So be kind to yourself, just believe you can do it."

Good luck

There we have it. The collected wisdom of my years of study, the thoughts of academics, my company's advisory panel, and your fellow students, all contained in the pages of a brief book.

I wish you all the very best in your study, and I'd love to know how you get on; just drop me an email: jon@aboutconsulting.co.uk.

And finally, to paraphrase one of my favourite film characters, "May the exam questions be ever in your favour!"

Acknowledgments

This book wouldn't have been possible without the support of very many people – to each of whom I'm incredibly indebted.

As always, Katie Murray wielded her editing pen with ruthless efficiency and kept me on track. I'd be lost without her. Jo Martin did what she always does and helped me find the words I was looking for, when my addled brain wouldn't play ball.

Sodiq Oyekola once again proved what a brilliant book cover designer he is, nailing the brief.

The tips and techniques in this book came from a wide variety of sources but special credit to my brother, Joe, who is one of the most passionate and committed educators I've ever met. He gave me some of the best revision techniques and deserves credit.

This book wouldn't have been possible without the huge support of Adam Owen and the NextGen Planners team. What an awesome and endlessly positive bunch of people to be around – I'm very lucky to be a part of it.

Finally, and as always, the biggest thanks to Madeline and the boys for being the best. Love you all millions.

About the Author

Jon Dunckley is a seasoned consultant, engaging speaker, skilled trainer, and accomplished writer. With over 30 years of experience, he proudly identifies as a geek! Despite an impressive educational background that boasts multiple degree-level qualifications across various disciplines, Jon is far from being a dull academic.

As the founding director of About Consulting Group (www.aboutconsulting.co.uk), he has earned a reputation for simplifying complex concepts to help the people he works with. Everything he does is based around a single mission:

"To help ordinary people achieve extraordinary things."

This goal is what drives him to share his knowledge every day, with as many people as possible.

Jon lives in Northampton with his wife, kids, and crazy dog, which keeps him fairly busy. In what little spare time he has, he competes in triathlons and generally looks for new ways to get into adventures...

Bibliography

Chapter one

1. Carraway, K. (2014) *Transforming Your Teaching: Practical Classroom Strategies Informed by Cognitive Neuroscience.* W.W. Norton and Company.
2. Mail Online (2012) *The boy who can't forget.* (Online) (Accessed 17/11/2023) https://www.dailymail.co.uk/news/article-2207642/The-boy-forget-Student-remember-did-ate-wore-day-decade.html
3. Wikipedia (2023) *Henry Molaison* (Online) (Accessed 17/11/2023) https://en.wikipedia.org/wiki/Henry_Molaison
4. Maguire, E. et al (2000) *Navigation related structural change in the hippocampi of taxi drivers.* Proceedings of the National Academy of Sciences. USA, 97(8) pp. 4398-4403

5. Jost, A. (1897). *Die Assoziationsfestigkeit in ihrer Abhängigkeit von der Verteilung der Wiederholungen.* Zeitschrift fuer Psychologie und Physiologie der Sinnesorgane, 14, 436-472.
6. Godden, D. and Baddeley, A (1975) *Context-Dependent Memory in Two Natural Environments: On Land and Underwater.* British Journal of Psychology, 66(3) pp 325-331
7. Mumford, Alan (1997) *Putting learning styles to work. Action Learning at Work.* Aldershot, Hampshire; Brookfield, VT: Gower pp 121-135
8. Barbe, W. Swassing, R. Milone, M. (1979). *Teaching through modality strengths: concepts practices.* Columbus, Ohio: Zaner-Bloser.
9. Dekker, S. Lee, N. Howard-Jones, P. and Jolles, J. (2012) *Neuromyths in education: prevalences and predictors of misconceptions among teachers.* Frontiers in Psychology. 3:429
10. Newton, P. and Miah, M. (2019) *Evidence-Based Higher Education – Is the Learning Styles 'Myth' Important?* Frontiers in Psychology, Volume 8.
11. Nancekivell, S. Shah, P. and Gelman, S. (2020) *Maybe they're born with it, or maybe it's experience: Toward a deeper understanding of the learning styles myth.* Journal of Educational Psychology. 112(2) pp. 221-235.

Chapter three

1. Buzan, T (2007) *Buzan's Study Skills: Mind Maps, Memory Techniques, Speed Reading.* London, BBC
2. HR News (2022) *Social Media: People can scroll*

the length of Mount Everest in 20 days! (Online)
(Accessed 13/2/2024) https://bit.ly/scrolleverest

3. Csikszentmihalyi, M. (2022) *Flow: The psychology of happiness.* Penguin Random House, London.

4. Tannock (2007) quoted in Carraway, K. (2014) *Transforming Your Teaching: Practical Classroom Strategies Informed by Cognitive Neuroscience.* W.W. Norton and Company

5. Pink, D. (2019) *When: The Scientific Secrets of Perfect Timing.* Canongate. London.

Chapter four

1. TheConversation.com (2019) *Would your mobile phone be powerful enough to get you to the moon?* (online) (accessed 2/11/2023) https://theconversation.com/would-your-mobile-phone-be-powerful-enough-to-get-you-to-the-moon-115933

2. Financesonline.com (2023) *90 Google Search Statistics for 2023: Usage and User Behaviour Data* (online) (accessed 2/11/2023) https://financesonline.com/google-search-statistics/

3. Jost, A. (1897). *Die Assoziationsfestigkeit in ihrer Abhängigkeit von der Verteilung der Wiederholungen.* Zeitschrift fuer Psychologie und Physiologie der Sinnesorgane, 14, 436-472.

Chapter five

1. Ferriss, Tim (2009) *Scientific Speed Reading: How to Read 300% Faster in 20 Minutes* (Online)

(Accessed 6/11/2023) https://tim.blog/2009/07/
30/speed-reading-and-accelerated-learning/
2. Rayner, K. Scotter, E. Masson, M. Potter, M and
   Treiman, R (2016) *So Much to Read, So Little
   Time: How Do We Read, and Can Speed Reading
   Help?* Psychological Science in the Public Interest
   2016, Vol. 17(1) pp. 29

Chapter six

1. Pauk, Walter; Owens, Ross J. Q. (2010). *How to
   Study in College* (10 ed.). *Boston, MA:
   Wadsworth.* Chapter 10: *"The Cornell System:
   Take Effective Notes"*, pp. 235-277
2. Mohsen Tahir Muslim Al-Mousawi, & Azel Adnan
   Faleh Al Saadi. (2023). *The effectiveness of the
   Cornell note-taking method strategy on Smart
   thinking among fifth grade female students
   (scientific section).* Utilitas Mathematica, 120,
   401–411.
3. Evans, Bradley. And Shively, Chris (2019) *Using
   the Cornell Note-taking System Can Help Eighth
   Grade Students Alleviate the Impact of
   Interruptions While Reading at Home.* Journal of
   Inquiry and Action in Education 10(1)
4. Akintunde, Oluyomi (2013) *Effects of Cornell,
   Verbatim and Outline Note-Taking Strategies on
   Students' Retrieval of Lecture Information in
   Nigeria.* Journal of Education and Practice. 4(25)
5. Quintus, Lori. Borr, Mari. Duffield, Stacy.
   Napoleon, Larry. Welch, Anita (2012) *The Impact
   of the Cornell Note-Taking Method on Students'
   Performance in a High School Family and*

Consumer Sciences Class. Family and Computer
Sciences Research Journal 30(1) pp.27-38
6. Buzan, T (2007) *Buzan's Study Skills: Mind Maps,
Memory Techniques, Speed Reading.* London, BBC
7. Reyes, E. P., Blanco, R. M. F. L., Doroon, D. R. L.,
Limana, J. L. B., & Torcende, A. M. A. (2021).
*Feynman Technique as a Heutagogical Learning
Strategy for Independent and Remote
Learning.* Recoletos Multidisciplinary Research
Journal, 9(2), 1–13.

Chapter seven

1. Oxford University (2023) *Plagiarism* (Online)
(Accessed 31/10/2023) https://www.ox.ac.uk/
students/academic/guidance/skills/plagiarism
2. Wikipedia (2023) *Ovsiankina Effect* (Online)
(Accessed 13/2/2024) https://en.wikipedia.org/
wiki/Ovsiankina_effect
3. Wallas, Graham (1926) *The art of thought.* New
York. Harcourt.

Chapter eight

1. Carraway, K. (2014) *Transforming Your Teaching:
Practical Classroom Strategies Informed by
Cognitive Neuroscience.* W.W. Norton and
Company.
2. Carey, Benedict (2014) *How we learn.* Macmillan,
London
3. Wikipedia (2023) *Zeigarnik effect* (Online)
(Accessed 17/11/2023) https://en.wikipedia.org/
wiki/Zeigarnik_effect

Chapter nine

1. Brinthaupt, T. M. & Shin, C. M. (2001). *The relationship of academic cramming to flow experience.* College Student Journal, 35(3), 457-472.

2. Kornell, Kate (2009) *Optimising Learning Using Flashcards: Spacing is More Effective Than Cramming.* Applied Cognitive Psychology, Volume 23, Pages 1298-1317

3. BBC News (2009) *Is it too late to cram for that big exam?* (Online) (Accessed 3/11/2023) http://news.bbc.co.uk/1/hi/magazine/8059860.stm

4. Sommer, R. (1968). *The social psychology of cramming.* Personnel and Guidance Journal, 9, 104–109.

5. Vacha, E., & McBride, M. (1993). *Cramming: A barrier to student success, a way to beat the system, or an effective learning strategy?* College Student Journal, 27(1), 2-11

6. Vogel, S., Schwabe, L. *Learning and memory under stress: implications for the classroom.* npj Science Learn 1, 16011 (2016).

7. Carraway, K. (2014) *Transforming Your Teaching: Practical Classroom Strategies Informed by Cognitive Neuroscience.* W.W. Norton and Company.

8. Hamilton, Nancy. Fresche. Ronald. Yichi, Zhang, Zeller, Gabriella and Carroll Ian (2021) *Test Anxiety and Poor Sleep: A Vicious Cycle.* International Journal of Behavioural Medicine. 28(2) P250-258

9. Huang, Sha, Aadya Deshpande, Sing-Chen Yeo, June C Lo, Michael W L Chee, and Joshua J Gooley. *Sleep Restriction Impairs Vocabulary Learning When Adolescents Cram for Exams: The Need for Sleep Study* Sleep (New York, N.Y.) 39.9 (2016): 1681-690. Web.

Chapter eleven

1. Peters, Steve (2011) *The Chimp Paradox – The mind management programme to help you achieve success confidence and happiness.* Vermillion, London
2. Bauer, Daniel Kopp, Veronika. And Fischer, Martin (2007) *Answer changing in multiple choice assessment – change that answer when in doubt – and spread the word!* BMC Medical Education 7:28
3. Poundstone, William (2015) *Rock Breaks Scissors: A Practical Guide to Outguessing and Outwitting Almost Everybody.* Little, Brown and Company.

Printed in Great Britain
by Amazon

44179741R00129